The Life Codes

The Life Codes

PATTY HARPENAU

JEREMY P. TARCHER/PENGUIN
a member of Penguin Group (USA) Inc.
New York

JEREMY P. TARCHER/PENGUIN
Published by the Penguin Group
Penguin Group (USA) Inc., 375 Hudson Street, New York, New York 10014, USA •
Penguin Group (Canada), 90 Eglinton Avenue East, Suite 700, Toronto, Ontario M4P 2Y3,
Canada (a division of Pearson Penguin Canada Inc.) • Penguin Books Ltd, 80 Strand,
London WC2R 0RL, England • Penguin Ireland, 25 St Stephen's Green, Dublin 2, Ireland
(a division of Penguin Books Ltd) • Penguin Group (Australia), 250 Camberwell Road,
Camberwell, Victoria 3124, Australia (a division of Pearson Australia Group Pty Ltd) •
Penguin Books India Pvt Ltd, 11 Community Center, Panchsheel Park, New Delhi–110 017,
India • Penguin Group (NZ), 67 Apollo Drive, Rosedale, North Shore 0632, New Zealand
(a division of Pearson New Zealand Ltd) • Penguin Books (South Africa) (Pty) Ltd,
24 Sturdee Avenue, Rosebank, Johannesburg 2196, South Africa

Penguin Books Ltd, Registered Offices: 80 Strand, London WC2R 0RL, England

Originally published in the Netherlands by The Life Foundation and Kosmos 2008
First published in the United States by Jeremy P. Tarcher/Penguin 2010
Copyright © 2008 by Patty Harpenau

Most Tarcher/Penguin books are available at special quantity discounts for bulk purchase
for sales promotions, premiums, fund-raising, and educational needs. Special books or book
excerpts also can be created to fit specific needs. For details, write Penguin Group (USA) Inc.
Special Markets, 375 Hudson Street, New York, NY 10014.

Library of Congress Cataloging-in-Publication Data
Harpenau, Patty.
The life codes / Patty Harpenau.
p.   cm.
ISBN 978-1-58542-803-8 (alk. paper)
1. Success—Religious aspects. I. Title.
BL65.S84H37   2010   2009051458
204'.4—dc22

Printed in the United States of America
1   3   5   7   9   10   8   6   4   2

This book is printed on acid-free paper. ∞

Book design by Jennifer Ann Daddio/Bookmark Design & Media Inc.

This is a work of fiction. Names, characters, places, and incidents either are the product of the
author's imagination or are used fictitiously, and any resemblance to actual persons, living or
dead, businesses, companies, events, or locales is entirely coincidental.

While the author has made every effort to provide accurate telephone numbers and Internet
addresses at the time of publication, neither the publisher nor the author assumes any
responsibility for errors, or for changes that occur after publication. Further, the publisher
does not have any control over and does not assume any responsibility for author or third-party
websites or their content.

For nothing is hidden that
will not become evident.

—JESHUA BEN JOSEPH

The codes are not effective if you ask for what you want,
but only when you sense that you already
have everything you are searching for.

Contents

· · · · · · · · · · · · ·

How to Read This Book

. . . .

Welcome to *The Life Codes.*

This narrative describes the journey on which I was shown the codes of life. They were taught to me by special teachers, and when you acquaint yourself with the codes, you will notice that you find quietude in your heart, happiness in your mind, and joy in your soul. The book describes seven days with seven codes. Seven teachers during your journey will teach you about the codes. At the end of each chapter you will find a brief summary, a question, and an explanation. You may choose to read it on the days of the week and to begin on Monday, or to first read all the codes and then return to the questions and explanations. As you progress, you can take a break to digest what you have learned and then, when you feel ready, return to where you were. Everything is possible. You can travel in whatever way feels good for you and make this journey as personal as you like. It does not matter how you travel, but that you travel. The only advice that I give you on your journey is to enjoy it.

For now . . . breathe steadily, install yourself on your couch with a cup of tea, and enjoy the journey. Allow yourself to be enchanted by the teachers in this book, and let their words warm your heart and permit your life to be changed by the codes.

Prologue

*Open your heart and mind, take my hand
and journey with me through seven wondrous days
with their seven codes, seven laws and questions.
May they inspire your mind and heal
and refresh your soul.*

—MICHAL BAT ABRAHAM

The room was dark. The rabbi's wife sighed in resigna-
tion. She was tired. It was extremely hot that day and the
energy in the room seemed to evaporate. The early evening smelled of fatigue. Rebecca, my teacher, clearly had
had enough of the endless stream of questions that I was
firing at her. She knotted her floral-print apron around her
waist, and I understood from this signal that she wanted to
return to her flock of children.

Rebecca was mother to eleven children and the wife of
one of the highest-ranking rabbis of the yeshiva. He taught
at a Jewish school of mysticism that was different from
most yeshivas. Rebecca's life was made up of homemaking
for her large family and extensive organization, because
the daily stream of guests who came to see her famous
husband was impressive. Many came from abroad, and an
even greater number came from within the country itself.

On Tuesdays and Thursdays, I took the bus from my

home to the Orthodox Jewish neighborhood, which was located not too far from the centuries-old center of Jerusalem. Directly opposite the bus stop was a modern coffee shop. The owner had by now become used to the fact that a European woman dressed in jeans, sneakers, and a T-shirt entered his shop, ordered an espresso, and headed for the toilet, from which a short time later she emerged in a long skirt and a long-sleeved cardigan, and wearing a scarf around her head.

During the first week, he eyed me guardedly. The second week, he stopped me in my tracks and demanded an explanation. From that day on he shared my secret. I studied kabbalah in the heart of Jerusalem, at the best and most controversial orthodox yeshiva. I do not know which he found more striking: the changing of clothes or the fact that a woman was studying kabbalah. He found it so amusing that he got my espresso together with a kosher sandwich ready as soon as the bus arrived at the stop. To guard my secret, I was given a special place behind the bar where I could discreetly stow my bag. I finished the espresso, saving the sandwich for lunchtime, and, my heart pounding, sneaked out of the coffee shop. I was afraid of being recognized. If someone were to identify me as a modern European woman, my studies would become history that same day. There was little risk, though, because the metamorphosis was considerable. And yet once I had turned the corner, I walked quickly along the pavement.

Every time I made the journey I would be met by a group of enthusiastic children halfway down the street—they seemed to tumble over me from all directions. I was hugged and made fun of because of my Dutch accent, and all the while my handbag would be brazenly emptied by the skillful fingers of the children looking for something tasty. The first thing to disappear was my lunch. If not enough could be found in my handbag, they also went for my pockets, and they quickly discovered the secret storage place in my knee socks. Rebecca's children warmed my soul, opened my heart, and filled my thoughts with love. The most precious moment, which always made my homesickness disappear, was the rubbing nose of her youngest child, Benjamin, who was allowed to use my sleeve as a handkerchief. However, as rapidly as they had noisily engulfed me, the children fell silent as we approached the school door. From the second stone onward, the laughter died and my child friends turned into wise little people.

They understood whose children they were and hid

their joy of life out of respect for those who found life more difficult. In the heart of this courtyard lived the rabbi with his family, and every day at the entrance a row of people could be found, waiting for words of healing, spontaneous miracles, wise counsel, or inspirational solutions.

Rebecca's fervent tapping interrupted my thoughts. It was clearly time for me to go, but something inside me refused. A wave of rebelliousness swept through me: I missed my country, I felt lonely and frustrated, and the lack of money was tearing me apart.

"Rebecca, this is not getting me anywhere," I murmured softly. She put her hand on mine and turned it palm up as if she were searching for a life line that could help her better understand me.

"Why don't you get married? Why don't you become the wife of a rabbi like me? I can see that you love children and you are beautiful. Do as I have done. Study in the back room. Listen to your husband and ask him your questions at the right time. There is nothing more I can teach you. You know all the rules for women, but your questions are those of a man."

At that moment, I understood her secret. She knew the answers, but she was neither allowed nor able to share them. It was her task to explain the rules, laws, and codes that Jewish women should follow in life. Further than that she could not go.

What a fool I had been! My ego had regularly whispered that she did not know the answers. I had created the illusion that I was smarter, because using my father's name I had secretly borrowed books from the yeshiva library, books that were not intended for women. Yet she had read them, just as I had; all of them and perhaps even more. Most likely with her heart pounding, in hidden rooms and at snatched hours, a secret covenant between her and her husband. "Does your husband teach you?" My question surprised me, and for a moment I thought she would be angry, but instead she stroked my head and left the room. The lesson was over. I felt confused. As if I had discovered a secret that I found I did not want revealed. I had not wanted to know that she was not allowed to share her knowledge with me. Her desire to protect the reputation of her husband was stronger than her desire to impart knowledge. I thought of all the women our history can boast of, those who were never heard or read, because they were women. How many of them over the centuries had hidden their wisdom? How many women had lost their dreams because they were not able or not allowed to show who they really were? From them were born the story women, wise women who knew the secrets of the soul, who smelled the breath of the universe and could find the light of power and explain the miracles of life. Throughout the centuries, they had been persecuted by the same kings and rulers who had first consulted them. Meticulously, they handed down their tales and knowledge to their daughters, hoping to make their stories the ambassadors of their hidden wisdom.

I sat in the yeshiva—the mystical heart of wisdom—and silently asked for all wise mothers in heaven to come to my aid. I could no longer depart without receiving an answer to my questions. I was not sure if I should leave the room, and just when I wanted to pick up my handbag and offer my apologies to Rebecca, the door opened.

The rabbi entered and sat down in the chair his wife had just vacated.

"So you are the Dutch woman with so many questions? I am told that you come by bus, change your clothes in the coffee shop around the corner, and twice a week are responsible for the fact that my children wait at the door like dogs wanting to play with you. I am told that you are not looking for a husband, but prefer to spend your time learning from my wife and asking her all kinds of questions. I have heard that you do not understand why you, as a woman, are not able or not allowed to study with the men in the yeshiva. I am not sure whether to be angry or proud that you are here. But if Hashem, the name of all—his name be praised—deems it necessary that you create an uproar in the heart of my center, then who am I to keep you from being here? Even if we are the mystic branch of Judaism and the chief rabbinate cannot decide if we are rebels or worthy of respect, you must know that I cannot allow you to study in the same room as the men.

"At the request of my wife, who apparently has great expectations of you, you will have me as your teacher. Once a week, you can ask me a question. One single question, no more. And for my part, I will disclose the codes to you on the corresponding days of the week. For seven weeks, I will expect you to be here on the correct day. We will begin on Monday, the day that Hashem projected his name into the universe and created his world. You must promise me, however, only to disclose the codes when I ask you to do so. You must swear on your father's name that you will accept the codes into your heart, and only when the ethereal breeze gives you a signal and I call your name in your sleep will you allow the codes, through your stories, to touch people's hearts. That must be your vow to me."

Never before had I felt so small and at the same time so proud. He sounded grumpy, but he was not. In his eyes I saw his appreciation for an honest searching. And searched I certainly had: in cupboards filled with words, in the shadow of each story and in the light of wisdom. I breathed a deep desire for knowledge, understanding, and wisdom.

Ever since my childhood days, I had bombarded my parents with all kinds of questions and, bellowing with laughter, my father had often ducked behind the couch, covering his ears.

"Enough, enough, you child of mine, go away, go play outside! Do as all other children do. Play!"

As if the rabbi had opened the window to my soul, the hidden thoughts came tumbling out, demanding to be heard. This wise man with his piercing eyes knew the art of opening each person's heart and listening. He received the confession of my search in loving silence. I told him the story of my childhood and my thirst for wisdom. I told him about the loneliness of my youth, about my strange and inexplicable dreams and my hidden secrets. At the time, I had not dared to tell my parents about them. There was too much fear of being found strange, or worse still, being rejected by them. Yet I had, on many occasions, seen a comforting look of recognition in my father's eyes. But still, I did not dare. A child in search of heaven seemed uncomfortably unusual.

With Rabbi Abraham I described things I had seen but could not explain. Tears choked my voice when I told him about the strange and profound melancholy that had always come over me like a grating emptiness in my heart, as if there were a hole in my heart. I had longed for something I did not know or recognize. It was beyond my comprehension, and it only added to the loneliness that kept me awake during the night, when the feelings inside me were too strong.

I sat, my mind filled with questions about life, as I searched for the answers. Who was I? Why did I exist, and where could I find God?

At school I was exposed to facts, knowledge, and science, but what I did not receive were lessons about life and the reasons for existence. Many a time in my life I would desperately wonder how life could best be lived and what, for heaven's sake, were the rules to live by.

In the year of my graduation my father died. The house was too big without him, and I fled from my memory of him. The grief I felt for him added to my wretchedness. I decided to go to Israel for a year, to study there and find a teacher. Then I had met Rebecca. At all costs, I had to discover what I was searching for; as my tears filled the space, it made the room go even quieter.

In his eyes I saw the flicker of recognition. Had I moved him or was I just imagining things? He seemed to recognize my loneliness and nodded affirmatively when I told him that upon reading one of his books—the contents of which I had for the most part not understood because of his way of juggling numbers and Aramaic letters—I had come close to literally falling over when I read the following words:

"In the book of creation, Sefer Yetzirah, God disclosed to Abraham the codes of life. If the codes are taught and understood, one can give shape to one's life."

This for me had been the sign I needed. From that moment I set aside every penny I earned, saving for my studies. At all costs I must go to this yeshiva, because a school where one was taught about life was the answer to my deepest longing. From those few words life had become lighter.

Hesitatingly, I asked the rabbi my first question: "The Abraham codes, do they really exist, and if so, what are they?"

He got up and smiled. "You are like my wife. She, too, does not leave me in peace." At the door he turned and said: "One code per week. No more. And one question as homework. We will start on Monday."

The God Code

The Law of Unity

For this is the matter from which
you were born.

I looked at my teacher. A friendly face with striking eyes. Eyes that were the color of the moon. He did not laugh much, and I understood his reserve, as aside from his wife, I was the first female student he had ever had. That morning I had come across Rebecca in the kitchen with her youngest child, Benjamin, on her lap. I was grateful to her and wanted to tell her this, but I saw the light of warm friendship in her eyes. It was not necessary. Things were fine as they were. She handed me a cup of tea and urged me to be on time. Ill at ease, I entered her husband's office. She called him Rav, the Hebrew name for rabbi. Rav Abraham. He was loved and feared for his knowledge.

"Welcome to your initiation in the first of the seven codes. You and I will journey through seven days, seven laws, seven questions, and seven teachers. Only when you have completed one code will you be introduced to the next one. I wish you a safe journey. You will notice that I use the word *God* in a different way from the one you are familiar with. The God whom you and I will discuss is the source of creation, a field of energy and a consciousness.

"Before introducing you to the miracle of life and of creation, I would like to give you a piece of wise advice. The codes that you are to receive in seven lessons are based on ancient knowledge, in fact the oldest knowledge in the world. It is abstract knowledge, the wisdom of the heart. As you know, there is both written and unwritten knowledge. It is the breath between the words that makes wisdom come to life. I would like to limit myself to this unwritten knowledge. This living wisdom with its codes of old is handed down from the teacher to the student. This is where you will have to make a choice. You can receive this knowledge with your mind. You will notice that as you listen, the inner voice in your head will ask you some tough questions. Your mind will immediately have an opinion or a judgment ready, because it is the activist, the impetus of human beings, and it will be eager to get going on the realization of why, when, and wherefore.

"The mind is more comfortable with codes of conduct than with life codes, and therefore I would advise you to give your head some rest. In the world of the codes there is no thinking. The codes need to be experienced."

The rabbi continued his lesson. "A melody is determined by the silence between the notes, and the same applies to the codes. They form the glue between all forms, the soul in all that lives. Your soul is already familiar with the codes. It is a code in itself. The soul knows who you are and why you exist. It will be happy to be acknowledged. However, it is your heart that will have to do the work. It is the heart's task to make a connection between the wisdom of your soul and the thinking of your head. Give your heart time to learn the codes, to feel and accept them. If you allow your heart enough space, you will find that it will automatically weave the threads for you between visible and invisible knowledge, between Thinking and Knowing, Being and Having. You will begin to live the codes as a matter of course.

"Think back briefly to a precious moment or a person whom you dearly love. Inhale this love. Can you sense how this thought opens your heart? Welcome to the world of love. Love opens your heart. You need this frequency to receive the words. Are you ready?

"At one time I learned from my teacher that everything you have is a reflection of who you are. This is true. Everything you have in your life is the result of who you are. Your convictions become your thoughts and your thoughts turn into deeds. It is a universal law that cannot be changed. You are where your attention is. Just as grass grows where it is able to grow, and if there is no space it will not thrive, so your life grows where it can grow, and if there is no space it does not blossom. In order to understand life you must understand the heart of creation, the foundation. In order to become adept at molding life and giving shape to life, you need to understand the clay that you hold in your hands. If you wish to live on the basis of abundance, love, and happiness, you will need to find the way to these frequencies.

"Abundance is not an object but a frequency, a field of energy, a consciousness. This field is reflected in matter. Drawn by your wishes and desires, the reflection of these desires is manifested in your life. It is important for you to understand this. People think in terms of what is concrete: in objects, matter, and everything they are able to make tangible with their senses. This has been taught to them by teachers who never ventured beyond what they knew. Someone who understands the universe, however, focuses on consciousness. Everything has a soul. The soul is the intelligence behind all that is visible. If you know people's souls, you know precisely what drives them and how you should deal with them. The same applies to forms and objects, because ultimately everything in the world of form is the result of thought. In the third code I will teach you more about this, but let us begin at the beginning.

"The first code begins with the soul of the universe and your own soul. You must go in search of your deepest desire and the reason for your existence. Without this you will lose your way in life and become entangled in questions about life: Who are you? What is life? What is death? Who is God? Who and what are human beings and what is the course of their life paths? The codes will also disclose your own path; they have done so for centuries. It is their task, for everyone, because the codes do not differentiate. They work because they were created that way. In the universe, everything fits together perfectly and each separate cog serves another.

"Life and death are codes, concepts, allegories, or references to the essence of our existence. In the same way God, heaven, and earth are also codes. Codes are secrets, hidden signs. In order to gain a better understanding of these codes, we tell each other stories in metaphors. The story of

Jeshua, to whom you refer as Jesus in Europe, teaches us the code of forgiveness. The meaning of the covenant of Moses teaches us the code of trust. Trust, such as unconditional trust ought to be. The first code, the God Code, teaches us unity, the clear and profound knowledge that everything is connected. For centuries, people have told each other fairy tales so as to gain a deeper understanding of life and to share experiences. From this, storybooks full of wisdom with beautiful folk tales and legends evolved. In Western narratives God is a man, whereas in other traditions and in certain ancient religions of wisdom, God has no gender. God is neither a person nor an object, but a consciousness. What is told in the Beginning of all Beginnings is a metaphor aimed at explaining the concepts of light and unity. Not an easy lesson, but for those who understand, it forms the indispensable foundation upon which all is built and will someday be.

"By understanding the metaphor of the story of the seven days of creation, you become acquainted with the path and the history of the universal soul. Know that your own soul is a perfect copy of this. The workings of the soul are also your workings!

"By teaching ourselves how to read the lines and shadows of words, spiritual concepts become clear and understandable, ready to use for each living being. However, caution is advised here: Within these codes, which form the essence of our lives, are contained extraordinary forces. Such forces can be used by people for the better but also for the worse. This is why these codes are frequently concealed. For the world of the mind and the ego they are hidden, but for a righteous soul they are easy to unravel.

"Each human being is composed of elements, namely heaven, heart, and mind. The task of the mind is to survive. The heart, with its intuition and feelings, guides one's life. The soul represents heaven with its characteristics and Godlike qualities. Each person has similar strengths, but not all human beings tread the same path. This is the basis of the game of life. The beginning and the end are the same for everyone, but the length of the path that lies between is determined by a unique code in the heart. Each human being has a code, a distinctive code with individual desires, paths, and lessons.

"We live our code. And this code is reflected on three levels: in a body, a personality, and a soul. The soul knows the way, while the personality determines the course and the body discloses the way and the choices made.

"This unique code can easily be recognized by each person, because it is nothing more than the deepest desire that each person carries within. It is the ardor in the heart, the passion in the soul, and all that makes each person take a deep breath. It is that which touches a human being most profoundly."

Who Are We?

"There is nothing secret about a secret. That is why secrets are created. Their aim is to uncover codes. We all adhere to the illusion that secrets are intended to remain hidden. The opposite is true, however. The difference between something that does not exist and a secret is the uncovering of it. Secrets wait patiently until one day they are disclosed.

"Once they have been stripped of all secretiveness, they provide answers. Life is not a secret and neither is death. God does not hide his world from people. People themselves throughout history have brought about a separation between God and Mankind, spirituality and beliefs. But there is no difference. All is one. There is no without and within, no above and below. All was created from the same breath. All that lives, has ever lived, and will one day live originates from the light.

"The laws of life and the accompanying codes represent a spiritual journey that each and every one of us has to make. They are the forces that one has to become acquainted with and discover in oneself, from the first until the last breath, and subsequently in a world where there is no physical breath but where nevertheless everything continues to live, the laws of life will continue to be in force.

"Once there was nothing. But nothing cannot get to know itself if nothing else is there. That is why the God Code was created, the first code of creation, Genesis, the story of how we came into being. The code of this story tells about how human beings, in the same way as God, are able to create through the power of thought. We possess the same characteristics and qualities as God. By projecting thoughts on the true-to-life universal screen, human beings follow God's example. On the first day of creation,

God projected his name in numbers, letters, and sound on the universal screen, and thus everything that lives, has ever lived, and will one day live became a reflection of his name.

"Come on, close your eyes for a moment: Who are you? Who are you really? Who are you when you have no name, no house or existence? If you have nothing left that makes you think of yourself, then you will feel a secret presence, a hidden consciousness, a depth in which you can lose yourself, because there is no other direction. Suddenly you are no one, and this is a confusing experience for the ego. Because who are you once you let go of your personality? Then you are nothing. Suddenly the screen of your life is blank. Then there is nothing but pure consciousness. Nothing . . .

"This is how it must have been on the first day. Everything was the same and there was no difference. No breath and no light. From this consciousness, the connection with all and nothing, that which we refer to as the God Code created life. The concept of God indicates energy, space, frequency, light, universe, soul of souls, heaven, higher self, everything, father, universal director, the All, power, or breath of all breaths.

"It is important for you and for all that lives to know that *you are this code. For this is the matter you were born from. This is your beginning. Your foundation."*

The God Code

As within, so without.
As above, so below.

"Once there was nothing. No beginning or end, place or time, no ever or never; an infinite field without borders, without a difference in light or darkness, in which light did not know how light it was. Simply nothing. An immeasurable world in which all and nothing were the same.

"At that moment, it dawned on God that he would never get to know himself if there never was anything else other than himself. He decided to give birth to temporality, and at that moment he engraved his name in the infinity of the universe.

"This was the first beginning. The separation between infinite and finite. Each one who would unveil the code of his name would understand the meaning: One is all, all is one.

"Then came the light with its planets and stars. Breathlessly God watched the light he witnessed for the first time. From that moment on everyone who managed to disclose the code would know that everything would remain in the light: For the light is me, I am the light.

"With his breath he made the heavens with its clouds and skies. So that everyone would know: I am heaven and heaven is within me. Then came the seas and the difference between light and darkness. The water from above was separated from the waters below. So that all life would know: I am life and life is within me.

"The uppermost heaven was filled with angels and in the bottommost heaven God placed the sun, the moon, and the stars. So that days and nights could be born and all that would float in the heavens would know: I am connected and everything is connected with me. On that seventh day all was ready for the living beings in the sea and in the sky to be born. And to them he gave plenty, so that with each breath they would know: I am God, and God is in me.

"On that day, for the first time God saw himself, and he rested. He laid down his head on mother earth and determined: I am everything and everything is within me."

THE FIRST PRINCIPLE:
THE LAW OF UNITY

I breathed a sigh of relief. The story of creation had come to life for me. No one had ever explained so clearly to me about the metaphor of creation and the meaning of the seven days, the seven codes, the seven metaphors, and the seven laws. The insight that the stories could be read as codes and metaphors came as a tremendous relief. Through the eyes of my teacher the phenomenon God began to dawn on me. The words "that day . . . God saw himself" touched me deeply. It was as if that day I, too, saw myself for the first time. In the darkened room and in the presence of my teacher, I felt a deep connection with every living being. At that moment, I learned that there is no you or I, and I knew intuitively that I formed part of something much greater. I felt a strong connection, a connection I had never before experienced. I regarded my teacher with surprise. Was he a rebel? A renegade? I had never heard a rabbi proclaim that human beings are equal to God. That creation had not taken place in seven days but on seven levels. My head felt like bursting, but my soul recognized the enlightenment of knowledge. I felt a huge sense of relief. This was precisely what I had been searching for. Ever since my youth until this very moment here in the heart of Jerusalem, I had been waiting for the moment at which I could disengage God from the white robe and the reproving finger. Open-mouthed, I continued to stare at my teacher; I had expected him to literally describe the first book of Moses, not for him to confirm my image of a loving and hopeful God. As if reading my mind, the rabbi explained to me that throughout the centuries many comments had been written regarding the Old Testament, and that, in particular, from the knowledge of the mystical books, such as the kabbalah, a lot of attention had been paid to the metaphors and the meaning of the codes it contained. He told me about the very first book of creation, Sefer Yetzirah. This book of creation tells of the mystical teaching that God whispered to the angels, who in turn passed it on to Abraham and Sarah, the patriarch and matriarch of humankind.

My teacher took my hand, and as if to comfort me, he addressed me using a Yiddish endearment: "Bubeleh, you are a child of God. Each of us is allowed to give our own meaning to his name. If you wish to see God as a light or energy, you are free to do so. You will find him in the wind, in the laughter of a child, in the seas and rivers, and in love. God is the breath that we breathe, the life force that we feel, and the current that carries us. That is why we have received the commandment: 'You shall not make an idol for yourself, whether in the form of anything that is in heaven above, or that is on the earth beneath, or that is in the water under the earth.' This commandment is a code. It means that you are free to use whatever image you have of God. No matter what the meaning of God may be for you. Precisely because there is no set image, we retain carte blanche to give free rein to our fantasy and to find him in everything we can see him in. You will find God in your own willingness to be like him. Every person is worthy, and you, too, live precisely that which you are. If you can teach yourself to give in to this feeling, you will blossom. From here you can allow yourself to be precisely that which or whom you wish to be. Because just like God, you are everything."

THE SECRET OF ALL SECRETS

For the first time in years my mind was quiet. The meditation exercise had a wondrous effect on me. The moment he had asked me to close my eyes, forget my name, my city and home, my parents and surroundings, my form and my personality, until I was nothing more than . . . consciousness—this experience could best be described as sitting without any sense of time, as if I was taken up in one great moment of silence. All my life I had listened to something, and in this moment I listened to nothing. This was a new experience for me. In that nothingness I experienced profound peace, a peace that I remembered from my childhood. It was as if I once again felt my mother's comforting hand on my head. Do you know that quiet sense of submission? That was precisely what it was, and it brought peace in my heart, mind, and soul. I would continue to do this exercise for the rest of my life. I had a clear understanding of the God Code. God is the story of who we are. Religion calls it God, science refers to it as quantum physics, and spirituality calls it light. We all mean the same, but we suffer from a Babel-like confusion. We were all made from the same stardust as everything we can see, smell, taste, hear, or feel. God's clay is made up of light, air, water, and fire. Everything that lives carries these elements within. Everything. This is the secret of all secrets: Everything is already there. Everything. No longer does anything need to be made. Nothing needs to be developed or thought out at the level of the soul. The soul knows that all abundance, love, prosperity, harmony, or whatever it is that we desire is already there. And this is where we come across the most important choice that we can make in our life. Do you look at your life from a soul level, a soul that knows that everything is connected? Or do you still live from the perspective that everything you long for still needs to be made? I know for certain that in heaven no baker of love who makes ten pounds of love per day is selective in handing it out. Everything is already there.

Abraham looked into my eyes. "You are there where your thoughts are, such is the law of life. The codes are not effective when you ask for what you want, but they are when you feel and know that you already have everything you are searching for." I nodded. I had understood the code. I decided to make the choice. I decided to be where I wanted to be. I would rely on the codes to teach me love, trust, and the way to wisdom.

GOD'S RADIO

The lesson had come to an end. Abraham left the room. He asked me to wait, because his wife still had a question for me.

On his way out, Abraham walked past an old radio. He turned it on, and I was surprised that he did not tune the radio to a specific frequency. A penetrating and unpleasant noise filled the room. After five minutes, I could no longer tolerate the crackling. Gambling on being caught, as I had not asked permission to fiddle with the radio, I nevertheless decided to turn the large brown knob and find the correct frequency. Relieved, I heard the crackling turn into a harmonious melody. At that same moment, it dawned on me: the radio! Of course, the radio! The God Code is a frequency. A frequency that an observant listener can tune in to.

I remembered having read this before: The old wisdom religions of this world and quantum physics teach us that everything forms part of a great field of intelligence, a field of infinite possibilities. In this field—which we refer to as God's world, the electromagnetic field, or universal intelligence—everything is composed of levels, frequencies, and wavelengths. There are lower frequencies such as fury, manipulation, grudge, anger, and jealousy, but there are also higher frequencies such as love, harmony, healing, and joy. Everything has a frequency. The radio is always turned on. Clear and distinct. It is not a matter of finding or listening to the right frequency. What matters is that the receiver is tuned in. Abraham's question to me was clear. "Wherever you wish to be is where your thoughts are. Where do you wish to be? Where do you wish to be in your life? What do you tune in to? If everything is already there, then where are you? Which frequency are you tuned in to?"

Question: Which Frequency Are You Tuned In To?
The First Life Code

The first code is the code of unity, and the code question that Abraham asks relates to the radio: If everything is already there, if everything is a frequency, then where are you? At which frequency do you live? Which frequency do you like tuning in to the most? Who are you? What makes you happy? Does abundance make you happy? Or do you prefer to live at the frequency of freedom? What inspires you the most and what is your innermost desire? In this universe, all frequencies are present. There are the lower frequencies of anger, grudges, manipulation, jealousy, and gossip. There are the higher frequencies of harmony, love, quietude, peace, happiness, and healing. If everything is already there, but you look at a world in which you do not see what you would like to see, then ask yourself which frequency you are tuned in to. What if you are in search of love? Love need no longer be produced. There is sufficient love for everyone. It is a law of life that everything begins with yourself. How loving are you toward yourself? Are you afraid of love? Are you able to share your love? Are you able to receive love easily? Are you attuned to love on an inner level?

Everything begins with yourself. Everything begins with awareness in your own life. Love encounters love when you yourself are love.

The word *love* can be replaced by any other word.

The Adam Code

The Law of Duality

In the world of light resides unity. The world
of air harbors the archangels. In the world of the
uppermost waters reside the angels and
on the earth live the people.

There is more to things than we realize.

It was Tuesday. Until a week and a day ago my world had consisted of time, this and that, places and events that existed apart and separate from each other. I lived in a world of forms and objects, differences and similarities, days and nights, seeming coincidences, unexpected joy, and a God in heaven instead of in my own heart. My heart understood the first code, but my mind was confused. At the end of the first day Abraham had asked: "Where are you?" The question about which frequency I was tuned in to had never been asked before. Just as with a radio, the idea of being able to find the channel for the frequency of unity was new to me. It sounded plausible and logical, but my mind and my ego asked my heart confrontational questions. The grandiosity of the range of possibilities that opened up for me at the thought of each human being carrying the characteristics and the qualities of God within was overwhelming and at the same time frightening. I understood that the codes could teach me to tune in to this frequency, and I decided to take the big step.

The Friday before, Abraham had telephoned me to wish me a peaceful Sabbath. He asked me whether I already knew the answer to the question. I asked him hesitantly if I could ask another question and, amused, he agreed. "Abraham, what does unity look like? What is the face of unity? How can I find the right frequency?"

"Bubeleh, use your imagination." He used the name that Benjamin had given me because he had problems pronouncing my Dutch name. Ben had found in me a partner in all that was sweet and edible. He called me Bubeleh because he found me sweet and kind. Before I knew it, this had become my pet name among the whole family. Later on they would change my name to an even shorter version: Bub. Sometimes Benjamin was allowed to go with me into the world outside. We then walked hand in hand down the street to the big, wide world. It was impossible not to fall in love with little Ben. As a child he led me by the hand, and I listened to his chatty explanation of how God had intended the world to be and how the angels once a year counted the clouds. He had lengthy explanations of the concept of time, and confiding in me, he told me the most curious stories about a clock that showed more than time. He knew this because at one time he had been a famous magician. I enjoyed looking at his cute little face, his bright eyes, his busy hands, and his brisk steps. Ben walked around with the world in his pocket and he used his imagination to explore anything he wanted. At night he could be found in ancient libraries reading the memory of the universe or he would go on a trip to India with his good friend *Donald Duck*. I was hopelessly lost when he looked into my eyes and said: "Bub, one more sweet, just one, because my heart needs something sweet."

"The most powerful tool a person has is the ability to imagine things. You are where your thoughts are. Do you remember? Unity has no image or form; it is a field. The power you need to enter this field is love. Love is a profound feeling; it is the soul of all that lives. Your essence is love. When you lead a loving life and regard life with the eyes of love, you automatically tune in to the right frequency. It is impossible not to find this frequency. There is no God other than God. All is already One. Use your imagination to find love in everything, because you encounter love when you are love. Imagine wearing glasses that only show you love. What kind of world would you then live in?"

I was thankful to him for his time, his patience, and the love with which he taught me. His family was the expression of love. From the beginning I had been accepted into the family as one of them, and to be honest, I could not imagine what my life was like before I had met them only a year before. It felt like I had known them forever. After our sessions, I often remained in the kitchen to talk with Rebecca. With admiration I looked at the large pans, the separate counters for the meat and dairy products. Their kitchen was kosher, and I learned to carefully handle the separate crockery. There was a cupboard with plates for meals in which meat was used, and another cupboard with plates for dairy food. The outside appearance was different from that of the family I had been born into. The sober clothing, the rich meals, the functional arrangement of the house were the complete opposite of the chic clothes of my mother, our rushed meals, and our large house. But on an inner level theirs resembled every other large family. There was arguing and laughter, teasing, and sometimes complaining. There was always a deep sense of respect. Everyone felt warm and appreciated. Words were used instead of punishment, and gossiping and lying were forbidden. The household felt safe and homey, so that often when I returned to my small apartment in the suburb of Jerusalem, I missed the family's voices and their laughter.

I knew there was no longer a way back for me. I walked the path of the codes. I had gone up the slide and had decided to start sliding. Actually, I had already made this decision earlier and had bravely gone up the steps. But because I did not know which way I would slide, I had hung on to the side. I did not dare slide, because I was afraid I might land in coldness and loneliness. Later on, life encouraged me to move forward, and yet I did not dare let go. Now I realized that I had been living in a world filled with fear of the unknown, without the confidence that I would always be in the right place at the right time if I dared to put my trust in life. I saw very clearly that life had never abandoned me. I had always had all that I wished for. In spite of all the love that it offered me, I still mistrusted life.

Abraham stopped talking, and for the first time he called me by my Jewish name. Apparently he had seen my father's name on my library card. According to Jewish tradition, you are named after your father, and thus I had been given the name Michal, child of Abraham, but was commonly known as Patty. "Good-bye, Michal bat

Abraham [Michal, child of Abraham], remember that you are life. You don't just have it, you *are* it. See you soon." The phone call had ended; I was left to mull over his words.

On Tuesday morning someone rang my doorbell at an early hour. Abraham's eldest daughter told me that her father was required elsewhere but that her mother had invited me for dinner. She had been told to deliver a letter to me personally. I thanked her and asked her to tell her mother that I would like to come at five o'clock. I opened the sealed envelope and immediately realized that I was holding the translation of an ancient manuscript. I closed the door and began to read.

The Abraham Code:
The Frequency of Duality

The light of God wandered across the earth. It smelled the sweet fragrances of the morning. It felt the warmth and the coldness of the seasons. It slept in the grass and played with the angels of the sea that God had named his dolphins. And God also wandered through the gardens of the earth, and in the heart of creation, there where the oldest roots of knowledge had dug out a way—in the soul of the world—God decided to rest. There he found Adam, his first human, and God saw his own soul reflected. "You are my Adam," God said. "You are me and I am you. The thought that I wanted to experience myself is the reason you exist. In the same way, any thought you have will also take shape, because you can create just like I can.

"I am all that is and you are a part of me. There was a time when you were just like me, but if you were all that is just like I am, you would not be able to experience life. Because I am death and life, light and dark simultaneously. But you, my Adam, are what you choose to be, and that is why I have separated you from my unity. The day needs the night to know who he is, just as life needs death to know that he is alive, and thus you, Adam, need to know what evil is in order to know who you are.

"Your world is a duality of opposites. From unity I have created everything in twos, so that you can choose and experience who you want to be.

"I offer you my house to live in. You are the king of my garden and the heart of my creation. You are the first human, and this is the visible world in which you live. This eternal Garden of Eden is yours. I give it to you unconditionally. You may do with it what you think is best. I give you the guardianship over all that lives, from the smallest to the largest, and it is your task to live life and then to return from the duality to my unity. But Adam, let me give you some advice: Never forget who you are and I will never forget you either. You are connected with me for as long as you choose to be. For this is my greatest gift to you, the free will to create whoever you choose to be.

"So that when the days are dark or light you will remember who I am, I will plant a tree for you. She is the oldest one in the world and I create her from my own soul. Her soil is the most fertile of all, her roots are the basis of all that lives, and her trunk contains all of life's secrets. You can rest in her shade and ask her for help or guidance. She is the tree of life that knows everything and connects heaven and earth. On her I will hang the codes for you and your offspring. They will glisten like sapphires from her branches. Know that each sapphire holds one of my qualities. They will show you the way on your life path. The codes are meant for you and all that is born from you, so that you will learn how to be the creator of the inner life. I pass on to you the wisdom of the codes of life, but be aware of the snake in the night because she carries the code of temptation. The codes contain lessons, and one of the codes will ask you to consciously choose for your soul. That is why you need the experience of temptation. The outcome of your choice is your free will, but still . . .

"If you should decide to one day part with the codes and forget them, you will lose the memory of who you are. Then you become a human without a soul and will be destined to die without remembering who you are. Then you will lose eternal life and once and for all you will continue living in and dying in the world of duality, and a heaven or a hell will be born for you until the day that you once again find the codes beneath the tree of all trees.

"Adam, for our souls there is no life or death, but for the world of duality there is a beginning and an ending. This is part of the experience of life. The temptation to choose what is visible, what we call life, might be great. It is the game between what is known and what is unknown, between fear and trust . . .

"That is why the first code, the code of Being, is the light of unity. I am the first code and you are the second code. I am One; the light and you are two, life.

"The light will put life to the test because life will

try to lure you away from unity with her luscious forms, whispered promises, and receptiveness to slumbering desires. You might regard her as eternal instead of temporal. Life will tempt you and whisper sweet words into your ear. For that is who she is. It is her job because she is your ego and personality. It is in her nature to rule, and she will open up her life fruits to you so that you will abandon the memory of who you are and choose her. Then you will lose your way in the world of duality. This, my child of all children, is the second code. Knowing who you are and knowing who you are not.

"You are the visible expression of the second code, for history and for the future, and that is why you live and die. In the meantime you will love life but also hate it. You will create but also lose and experience the greatest pleasure and the most profound unhappiness. This is all that you will be. All of it. You are the difference between good and evil. This is what you stand for. You are the code of the personality and the ego. Such is the code of your name, because Adam stands for life.

"So as to let you experience life, I am detaching myself from you. You will be naked there where you go so that you know that you will be dressed in my love. And only then, when you shed the garments of love, will you be besieged by shame and darkness. No sooner than that. Only when you make that choice.

"As long as you live, we will for this time not be alike, but nonetheless eternally equal. So that you will remember me, I am planting my name of unity in your heart and you will be able to hear me in the silence of all that is. Be still and know that I am with you. You will meet me in the silence. Close your eyes and think of me, and I will find you. This is my vow to you.

"If you lose your way from the garden of love, then remember my name and you will find me again, even in the darkest moment of your existence. You need not ask me anything. I am your equal. Do not build an altar for me because my chair is your chair. Do not build me a house, but share your gifts with those who need them. You need no other prayer than the prayer of yourself, and the place that you need to turn to me is within your own body.

"Each code contains a name with which you can connect and find the frequency. My name gives you the power to create because my power and my qualities live in you. I created the world by writing my name in the universe. You may use my name to create what you think is needed, so that it is good and sacred. My name is also your name. But remember that you shall not use my name, the name of your God, idly. For I shall not maintain the innocence of those who use my name idly. You have the responsibility to know what you say and do in my name. Good or evil is your choice, but know that all that you create in your life, you will certainly encounter. According to the law of life, all that you see, feel, speak, and do will rebound.

"As within, so without. Just as you are a visible expression of me, everything that you say will become a visible expression of your thoughts.

"Speak my name in silence using the force of your breath, because you were made from my breath. Find a peaceful place and breathe my name while you inhale and exhale. Your soul will recognize the sounds because I have engraved the code of my name into these four sounds. My name is JHWH. The soul between the consonants is the sounds A and E. Slowly inhale JAH and hold the sound with your breath for a moment. Then breathe out the sound WEH to the outside world. Between the inhalation and exhalation, you will see in your imagination who you want to be."

The Code of the Past

The manuscript lay in my hands. I carefully closed my eyes. I had never prayed before. I had never known or found the right words. In the silence of my room, I began to breathe. I slowly breathed in the sound JAH and breathed out the sound WEH. I let my breath automatically do the work. After all, it knew better than I how I should breathe. In the beginning I experienced discomfort and now and then even got a bit out of breath. But as time went on, a sense of peace slowly came into my heart, one that I had never before experienced. At a certain moment I realized that for a time no thoughts had entered my mind. I felt a space that I had only felt at moments when I had been speechless or deeply moved. I felt the tears trickle down my cheeks without understanding why I was so touched. My heart filled with love and trust and it became lighter than ever before. The Adam Code had opened up a new world for me. The first code had taught me about the clay of the universe. Everything, visible and invisible, was made up of the same energy or light. The second code made me conscious that, in spite of the fact that we are all One, we need a life and a personality to experience ourselves. I had been complete all the time without realizing it. I had left the Netherlands to go in search of myself. In search of who I already was.

Life is a game of duality. If there were no differences, then it could not be experienced. Happiness exists by the grace of misfortune, and this realization made me take a piece of paper and draw a bold line down the middle. On the left side, I sketched some boxes in which I noted my unhappiness and all the painful lessons life had taught me. On the right side, I filled the boxes with happy and loving experiences as well as my most precious moments. The connecting thread in my life became visible, and suddenly I very clearly saw which character traits, qualities, and experiences I had learned from my mother. I did the same with my father. In a neutral way, I looked at my life lessons, and what I saw was the map of my past. It was as if a burden fell off my shoulders. The insights involuntarily began to tumble into my thinking. I began to discover a route through the connection between the one part and the other. I was in the middle of the story of my life, and my heart pounded in my throat. I saw my youth and wrote down my biggest sorrow and my greatest happiness and thought back to Abraham's question: "Where are you? What do you attune to?"

The Garden of Life

It was time to go to Rebecca. The children would already be standing at the corner waiting for me. When I walked into the street, the youngest looked at me with his dark brown eyes. I recognized the moon in those eyes. He resembled his father. Benjamin lisped with his tongue between his changing teeth: "Abba iz abroad. He had to leave. You have no lezzon now and I'm zure you want to play with me and my marblez." I saw the love in his eyes and felt how his little hand wanted to grasp mine firmly. I put my arms around him.

A few months back I had been sent a large bag of marbles from the Netherlands, and I had taught the children how to play with them. I kissed his nose and decided to first ask his mother if she could use my help. Rebecca was standing in the kitchen. Steam was coming from the pans and she was busily occupied. "I am busy," she said, and pushed me back into the hallway. "Go on, there's a teacher waiting for you. Be quick, because we will be eating at six o'clock."

"Rav Abraham is on a trip. You should have received a letter this morning." A tall dark-haired man looked at me inquisitively for my answer. "My name is Adam. It will be clear to you that because of my name, the second code is my specialization. The name *Adam* means 'human' or 'life.' I am at this yeshiva temporarily to study the book of creation, Sefer Yetzirah. I am a Christian by faith and I also work as a landscape gardener, but only when I am not called to work for Rav Abraham. He likes to use me, you see, to teach his students the principles of sowing and reaping. As it is, the Adam Code and the garden of life are metaphors for the process of creation. The first code teaches us about the possibilities that our own garden provides. The second code teaches us that we may use this garden and cultivate it as we wish.

"But which seed do we wish to plant? The tallest tree is born from the smallest seed. What determines the visible results is that which an individual plants. What is the seed made up of? The seed finds its strength in the longing that it carries in it.

"Is what we plant really what we want? Do the contents

of our seed consist of our wishes and desires, our greatest sense of lack or our deepest longing? What is our life really about, and what is our highest and most precious good? When a human being knows its longings and is willing to plant them into the emotions of the heart, then the seed will grow into the visible expression of an invisible longing.

"The Adam Code teaches us that we not only have a soul but also an experience. We are in this life to experience ourselves, and that which we wish to experience is connected to our deepest longing. After all, you want to be who you long to be, right? That is why we are here. We are here in the garden of life to plant our deepest longing, whatever it may be. Do not plant based on a hope or a wish, because that will keep you hoping and wishing. That which you sow, you will reap.

"Accept what a landscape gardener is telling you: Never plant your sense of lack because if that is what you sow, you will plant into barren ground. But if you plant what you truly experience in your heart and are open to receive it, you are planting in fertile ground. A gardener plants and does not doubt for a moment that his wishes will blossom. Everything already is, after all."

I looked at him pensively. "How do you pretend it is already there even if you do not have it yet?"

He smiled approvingly. "Use the first code. Everything already is. The world of objects and forms is an outer expression of the inner world of your thoughts. Everything you can see, smell, taste, touch, and hear at some point began with a thought. To your soul everything already exists because you know that you form part of the field of unity. Plant from this wisdom in your heart. In silence go to the garden of life in your heart. Slowly begin to inhale and exhale to the sounds JHWH. Plant your deepest longing between the inhalation and exhalation of these sounds. Use the power of your imagination. In your imaginary garden your desire is present and visible.

"A wise gardener begins by knowing his desires. They are the seed of his thoughts. Then he makes certain that he is working with fertile soil. The soil of trust is that everything already is. He proceeds by following Adam's example because he knows that he has a right to grow whatever he wants. He has the right of free choice, and in this ground he plants his seed. Then he lets go of his desire. This does not mean that he does not care whether or not it will grow. His trust is so great that he is certain that it will grow. He just lets nature take its course. Things grow as they should grow. In accordance with everything he plants, one half will appear and the other half will not. Such is the law of life. One thing exists by the grace of another. From the hundreds of seeds he plants, half will emerge, and this is the choice he has: Does he keep focusing on that which does not grow or on that which flourishes?

"He does not judge that which is not and will not appear. He remains neutral. That which does appear is greeted by him with gratefulness and passion. He takes what he needs and shares the rest in love. This is how a wise gardener works. It relates to flowers and plants but also to wishes and desires. Rav Abraham wonders what you would like to sow."

It was clear to me that the time had come to enter the garden of my life. I should have known. First I had become acquainted with the creator of the garden. Subsequently, with the earth. And now the time had come to sow. My head was tired and empty. Best to continue tomorrow, and I was happy to be called to the dinner table by the children. I thanked Adam, the universal gardener, for his lesson. Holding the door handle, I turned around once again: "I miss Eve. Where is Eve in this story?"

What Is Your Past, What Is Your Future?
Living the Second Code

The second question that Adam, the universal gardener, asked was: "What do you wish to sow?" A wise gardener starts by knowing the desire: the red line between past and future. That is the seed of his thoughts. What is your deepest wish? What is your deepest desire? What is your highest good? Imagine standing in front of an immensely big mirror, a mirror that shows you the most beautiful personal moment of your life. Where do you then stand, and what are you doing? Close your eyes for a moment and imagine standing in front of this mirror. The mirror is showing you the outcome of your deepest desire. What do you see? How does it feel? That is the feeling that you must plant in the garden of your heart. You plant it by living it.

We humans are made up of three layers: a physical layer with forms and objects; a sensing layer with feelings and thoughts; and a causal layer with a soul and a desire to create. There is a law in this life that says that energy attracts congenial energy. This means that behind each form lives a deep longing. This deep longing is a very strong energy. What matters is not that you wish for the object but the feeling behind the object. For example: A car is a steel container on four tires. And yet when you think of your car, you think about the feelings that it elicits: freedom or security. Humans do not think in terms of objects but in terms of desire, and these desires reside in your heart, not your head.

The Eve Code

The Law of Desire

And God created man in His own image.
In the image of God he created male and female.

*For where your treasure is,
there your heart will be also.*

—JESHUA BEN JOSEPH

*Note to the reader: Take a pen and a large
sheet of paper, and if you like, join in
the journey with the next story.*

I dreamed that I was awake. I had woken up and walked out of the window. Not just like that, because I would have fallen.

In front of the bedroom window I saw a floating staircase. Carefully I put my foot on the first step and automatically the other steps followed upward. I walked through the air, and in my dream it was a very normal thing to do. It was a large staircase. A staircase leading into the clouds. With each step I felt myself becoming lighter, and when I had reached the final step, I carefully jumped onto a bed of clouds high up in the sky. There I saw a door. A floating white door, and I heard voices softly singing. I wondered whether I had ended up in heaven, but at that same moment I noticed someone standing next to me. He was not old, and yet he felt far from young. His skin was smooth, but I was looking into the oldest eyes in the world. He nodded to me amiably and put me at ease. He told me that I was in the topmost element of the earth, and indeed, I saw how we were surrounded by the most beautiful clouds. The light softly played through the layers of nebulousness and it was breathtakingly beautiful. "Where am I?" I asked.

"You are in the land of desires. In this land all dreams and desires are stored. This is the place to which all wishes are brought and fulfilled. The people of the lowermost elements think that they make up their desires, and that one day they will wake up with a deepest wish and then set out in search of its fulfillment. But actually it is the other way around. Here in the land where all dreams reside, desire searches for a heart that is willing to listen." He noticed my surprise. It felt as if the world had been turned upside down. I had never looked at it this way. "You mean that we humans are the expression of what we long for?"

"Every human being who decides to live a life carries a longing with them in their heart. A collective longing to learn to become love in a world that you call the earth. But in addition, each human being also carries an individual desire. This desire will become visible during one's lifetime. This is why you think that you have desires, whereas in actuality you are them. Let us do an exercise." We had come to a large board in the sky and he handed me a transparent pen. "If you wish, you can write your deepest desire on this sheet of cloud paper. Ask your heart what you wish for most and write it in golden letters on the clouds." I did not have to think for long. I wrote my deepest wish in golden letters in the universe. It felt wonderful because right there in golden letters was written my wish.

"Ask your heart a second question. What is your greatest sense of lack? What are you looking for the most?" Next to my deepest desire I wrote my greatest sense of lack. Together we looked at it and I was surprised that they were essentially the same. They stood right and left from each other and were each other's opposite. That which I most desired was also what I missed most.

"Are you ready for the next question?" I nodded. "Next to your deepest desire and your greatest sense of lack, write your unique talent. Each human being has a unique talent. This is not something you do or know. It is a unique quality that is so taken for granted that you do not even realize that it is your greatest good. The people around you are aware of it because it makes you who you are to them. Ask them what makes you unique and you will have the answer to my question."

I closed my eyes and with my thoughts I asked my best friends what they considered my greatest talent. In a soft whisper I heard the word *love*. As if he were able to hear my thoughts, he nodded approvingly. "Each human being works with love. It is the collective desire, that which binds us. We are love, and that is why it is our highest good but also that which we miss the most. But besides love, what is your unique talent? I can help you by showing you that it has no form. It is the feeling you give people if you love them. This is what you want to share with them the most. It is the energy that people look for in you at the times that they are searching for the soul of love. It can be appreciation, the capacity to offer attention or to listen. It can be unconditional giving, acceptance, or empathy. To you this special ability is the most natural part of you, because you are it, and this is the code of your life."

I asked my heart, and it knew the answer. Next to my desire and what I missed most, I wrote my talent in large letters in the sky.

Once again I saw the connection linking these three words.

"We are almost done. Only two final questions. A nice one and a difficult one, but you will find that they can teach you a great deal. Let us look at why you are here in the experience you call life. What is your life's lesson? What is the theme of your life? When you run into obstacles in your life and life hands you a difficult lesson to learn, what do you look at? What is the lesson you must learn? Which experience are you regularly confronted with in different situations?"

In the reaches of my memory I saw the ghosts of painful and difficult experiences. Helped by the energy of the one who was guiding me, I saw that they had been tests of strength. At times I had recognized the lesson and sometimes I had not. I had avoided it, stumbled over it, and I saw that it showed up for as long as it took me to muster the willingness to look at it and learn from it.

Next to my desire, my sense of lack, and my unique talent, I now also wrote down my lesson. I saw the connection and fell silent. I began to see what my life was all about. My longing was also the lesson I had presented to myself in life.

"Here is the last question: What is your purpose? What do you want to achieve? What is the driving force behind all your actions? What is the fuel of your soul, your passion?"

I needed to sit down for a moment to think about it. Once again I asked my heart and felt it pound. By knocking on the door of my heart, I felt how my stomach woke up and my ambition began to flow. What did I actually want to achieve? What did I really want from my life, and what would make my life truly successful? At first I saw only shapes and objects in my imagination, but the tangibility slowly faded into a deep feeling I had always searched for.

Once again I regarded my desire, my sense of lack, my talent, my lessons in life, and suddenly I saw my life's purpose brightly and clearly appearing in the sky.

I was now also able to decipher the last piece of the code. I wrote the last word in golden letters in the sky and saw the connection.

"Look at your words. Look at your desire, your sense of lack, your talent, and your passion with its purpose. The greatest secret that you can discover in your life is that you already are everything. You already are. Now, at this moment. Not in a while, not one of these days, not later.

But now! Bring your attention to your heart and give yourself permission to see who you, by nature, already are. You have no desire, but you are it. Everything is stored in the core of your soul, and you live life with the purpose of making this core of your soul visible. However far away your goal may seem, you are it already because otherwise you would not have this desire. People do not long for things they cannot, or do not, want to be. This is the secret of all secrets. That which you are is what you automatically will live. That which you want, you find by being it. So in a while, wake up, look into your own eyes, and say to yourself: 'I am all that I am.' Keep repeating this until you trust that you are indeed just that. Sing it in the morning, whisper it during the day, embrace it in the evening, and take it with you in your sleep. You are what you are because you are everything. You may be everything because you live in Adam's garden and in Eve's soul."

I woke up with a start. What a strange dream. My life seemed filled with teachers. I told Abraham on the Wednesday when we saw each other again. He had returned from his trip, and I noticed the circles of fatigue under his eyes. He worked hard, and it had become clear to me that many people came to visit his soul. I told him about my dream, and he listened attentively while he poured me a cup of fresh mint tea. I asked him about his deepest desire, and it surprised me that he gave such an honest answer.

"Each human being searches for love, including myself. The most beautiful gift is the meeting with my wife and children. But there were times when love did not live in my life. I am from a small village where large families had to share a lot with each other: the land, the harvest, but also the threat of evil. It was a cold youth with short and lonely nights. My mother worked the land and my father traveled from village to village to tell his stories. He was a story man, and in the suitcase of his memory he had stories for the soul, stories of love and strength, but also of healing and wisdom. His stories are well known all over the world. They were passed down and put on paper, but he himself did not manage to earn money from them. As a child he advised me to guard his stories carefully because there would come a day when I would benefit from them. And indeed, I always have a story at hand to explain the codes of life. The rough journeys he made in order to tell his stories in all corners of the world were the reason that I had to take care of the family and that there was no time for myself. I did not learn the art of love for myself, and searched for my greatest solace in stories and books. My greatest desire became the search for an abundance of wise words. In the mirror of life I saw the expression of this desire. Life gave me a school filled with mystical stories and plenty of wise words. But deep in my heart I knew that I was searching for the appreciation that I had so wanted to get from my parents. In my soul I know that they, may they rest in peace, loved me, but the ears of a child want to hear the words. The deepest sense of lack in my life that is written in my soul is the absence of appreciation when I was young. According to my loved ones, my greatest talent is expressing appreciation. And indeed I think that by teaching people through the codes, I can teach them how to meet themselves, because knowing who you are gives you inner strength and peace. I am also strongly convinced that, once you understand the path of your life and follow this path, you will be accompanied on your way by the energy of abundance. Each morning when I rise, I tell myself that I am appreciation. Believe me when I tell you that it has taken a long time before I could embrace the feeling that I was allowed and able to live this. When the codes crossed my path and I understood who I truly was, I dared to look at myself in the mirror one morning and was able to speak the following words accompanied by the strength of appreciation: 'I am all that I am.'

"Bubeleh, the codes are magical. When you invite them into your life, you will find them everywhere on your path. They are rightfully the life codes. They actually are alive. They whisper their wisdom in your dreams, in the people with whom you live, in the wind in the street, and in the situations you encounter. The code of life is that it speaks to you. Because you are the code, and the best place to meet life is in yourself.

"I have brought a story for you. You have already answered this week's question. You know who you are."

The Eve Code

It was on the longest day that God traveled back to heaven. He was proud of his earth. He saw the new wheat blowing in the wind. He heard the bees hum while they carried out their pollinating work, and he smiled at the sight of all this business. He saw his glimmering fish children play in the clear blue waters. He caressed the white beaches and here and there blew a rippling in the mosaic of the water. What appealed to him most was the rippling pure water from the mountain, so perfect with its greenish glow. He smelled the herbs and the soil and, enraptured, watched the splendor of color. It was good as it was. He had not wanted it to be any different, and he left. He traveled through stars and times. Now and then he stopped to enjoy the view, and a number of years past the moon he came to a forgotten corner. He would have passed her if she had not called out to him. He heard her voice and, entranced, continued to listen to it.

His senses were ignited at the sound of so much beauty.

She had already observed him for some time, from a distance. She knew very well who he was. She had watched his actions and seen him fly. She knew how he built and contemplated. And with amusement she had waited for him to find her. He had almost flown past her, and she understood that one cannot see things one has never seen before. She lowered her voice a bit so that he could not hear her, and she waited quietly until he was able to see her.

"Who are you?" he asked her.

"Who are you?" she asked him.

"I am God. I am everything."

"Oh," she said, "I am nothing."

Her answer surprised God. He realized that he had come up against a dilemma: He was everything and therefore also nothing. Who might she be if he was everything and nothing?

She noticed his surprise, and the sound of her laughter sparkled through the universe. At that moment, God fell in love. So hopelessly lost in love that for the first time he felt his own longing. He grasped his chest, and in the emptiness between his ribs, he felt something throb that resembled his heart but was somewhat different. At that moment, a bit more in the middle behind his ribs, the loving heart of God was born.

The angels heard it for the first time and stopped working. "What sound is that?" They put their ears to the clouds to listen. And sure enough, a consistent rhythmic beating could be heard. They followed the sound and finally found God who, his cheeks flushed, had laid down his head in the lap of his Goddess.

It became busier and busier. The space filled with gestures and sounds, and it was as if the light shone everywhere. When she began her story, everything fell quiet. Heavenly quiet.

. . .

"One day there was everything. There was only light. Everything was the same. Everything and nothing was One. Unseen and unknowingly this light multiplied until it had become infinite and immeasurable. On that day, the longing was born to experience light. And thus the consciousness of the universe awakened and understood that it must separate into two forces: a force of sharing and a force of receiving. This is how the intelligence of the universe was divided into love and light. And that is how you, my God, were born like a child of the light. By letting your light shine, the world became visible. The world was already there, but for the first time someone had switched on the light. Thus you shone across the heavens and the earth; you fueled the stars, and the sun and moon filled up with your power. Everything that at first had lived in the dark became visible through your power. I am your Sophia, the feminine and divine part of you. We were born from the same light, the same as you on the same day. I am love as you are light.

"Together we form the nature of the universe. I want to share everything in love, and that is why everything in this infinite field serves something else. You are the visible part of me. You are the forms and the objects, the creator of all that can be seen. But I, my dear God, I am the creator of that which is invisible. I am the substance between the tissue and the breath between life. You are the soul of souls, and I am the heart of hearts. I am the longing that awakens you to search for fulfillment. You are the giver and I am the receiver. You and I together are Ish and Isha, the yang and yin, a masculine and a feminine energy contained in one body. You need me to know what your heart desires, and I need you to build. You and I fit together perfectly. I live in you and you in me.

"You must still return to the earth. Do not forget. You have shown your Adam, the code of masculine energy, how to see himself. But the code of femininity in Isha, the female human, must still be illuminated. She continues to live in the dark until you show her. Then Adam can find his inner Eve and discover the heart of love. But know that she will seduce him with the apple that is handed to her, because she embodies the code of transformation and birth. Together with her snake, she carries the code of physical temptation. So that humans can enjoy their nakedness and can copulate in love, free of shame and with pleasure.

Thus Eve will bear children and populate the world with hearts and souls that share one another in love. She is the visible expression of me. She will let her love shine.

"On that divine day, God shed light on the women of the world. The world was in balance. Men and women found each other and built an ark filled with life. For each one a counterpart, and for everything a force to be shared and a force to receive in love. This is how it was written in the stars. That day, Eve became visible for the first time.

Who Are You?
Living the Third Code

The purpose of this third code
is to find the code of your soul.

QUESTION 1: WHAT IS YOUR GREATEST DESIRE?

In the previous chapter, you stood in front of the mirror of your desire. If you wish, you can write down your answers.

QUESTION 2: WHAT DO YOU LACK THE MOST?

What is missing in your life? What has ever been missing? The answers to the first and second questions probably are not far apart. They are most likely the plus and the minus of each other. For example: My deepest desire is to be seen, and my deepest sense of lack is when people do not see what I am capable of or what I do.

QUESTION 3: WHAT IS YOUR GREATEST TALENT?

Recognizing your own talents is like looking around in a dark room. Ask a number of people who know you well what they think your greatest talent is. Then look at the connection among your desire, the lack you experience, and your talent. Carefully examine whether you can discover a link among these answers. Often there is one between your deepest desire and that which you lack the most. They are the plus and the minus of the same energy. Your talent is the tool with which you can fulfill your desire.

QUESTION 4: WHICH ARE THE LESSONS YOU ARE APPLYING?

Which painful experiences and lessons cross your path time and again? Which obstacles do you run into? If someone tramples on your heart, which lessons are you then shown? Life teaches us lessons, and we come across teachers who show us what we should do but also teachers who show us what we should not do. They test our inner strength, perseverance, or ability to have faith in ourselves. Put this answer next to the others and see if you can find a link.

QUESTION 5: WHAT IS YOUR PURPOSE IN LIFE? WHAT HAVE YOU GOT TO SHARE?

You should now be able to see the recurring themes in your life. Your deepest sense of lack, your greatest desire, your talents, and your lessons help you find the purpose of your life. If it does not become clear immediately, then ask someone to tell you what they think, or quietly continue reading and repeat the exercise at a later time.

Intermezzo

Letter to the Reader

Jerusalem, Winter 1983

Dear Reader,

With my words I take you with me to Jerusalem in the winter of 1983, on December 19.

On that night the telephone sounded loudly through my sleeping apartment. Barely awake, I found my way to my telephone. Hesitatingly I picked up the receiver, filled with a sense of apprehension. I heard the worried voice of Abraham and had difficulty recognizing his familiar sound. "Can you come and fetch Ben? Rebecca has been urgently admitted to the Hadassah Hospital. The older children will remain at home, the little ones will go to the neighbors, but Ben refuses to go anywhere except to you. He is now still sleeping. Can you take the first bus?"

My heart stuck in my throat. I asked him how serious it was. "It is not good news, Bubeleh, not good. The doctors are fearing the worst, but we will know more by morning."

Sleep had left me and I was filled with an unfamiliar fear. I cleaned up the house to kill some time, I made up the guest bed for Ben, and made a call home, to the Netherlands. My mother's voice filled me with tears, and for a moment I was able to become a child again.

I realized how much I had become part of Rebecca's family and how much I had come to love them. Nevertheless, nostalgia continued to be my unwanted friend. I missed the familiarity, the fragrance of remembrance, and the taste of invigorating winters. A year before I had left for Israel, my father had died. My mother could not bear the memories of him and moved into a new house. I then lost the house I had grown up in. I lost my bearings when I lost my little room, the old kitchen, and the safety of my youth. Just like my mother, I had taken flight—to Israel—and I had promised her that I would not be gone for more than a year. The year became longer. But the moment I heard her voice on the end of the line, everything came flooding back. My mother was my home. Wherever she was. I heard her comforting words and her offer to come over. "No, not just yet. I will call you later once I know more."

The first bus that morning drove slowly and it seemed to take hours before I arrived in the heart of Jerusalem. My good friend was sweeping the sidewalk in front of his coffee shop and raised his shoulders in surprise when he saw me there at the crack of dawn. At that point I had stopped changing my clothes there, and my secret friend had by then become used to my skirts and colored stockings. Just like Rebecca's unwed daughter, I wore my hair in a thick ponytail.

Each week I drank my familiar espresso at his place and told him about my secret life with Rebecca and her family. Even though they did not know each other, they had become good friends from a distance. He met her family in my stories, and her family got to know him through the endless stream of cookies and tea that he faithfully handed to me for them. The generous gifts were received with joy. I did not speak openly about the lessons with the Rav, but the change in me had not gone unnoticed by him. That morning he could tell by the look on my face that I was worried, and he ran after me with comforting words and cookies for the children. At the front door of the house, people had already lined up to wait, quiet, worried, and with modesty. Some wanting to wish well, others with prayers or with a silent longing to be close by. Rebecca was loved down to her very soul.

Apparently Ben had been on the lookout for me, and he came storming out of the house. "We have permission to go to the zoo, and tonight I can sleep at your place! But I did have to promise Abba that we would call home very often." I hugged him and asked him to go and fetch a sweater. Then I walked into the Rav's office. There I found Sarah, the Rav's secretary, her eyes red from crying. Abraham was still at the hospital and the oldest children had joined him there. The house was quiet and sad. I did not dare to walk into the kitchen. I did not want to feel Rebecca's absence. Sarah asked me to call every two hours in case there was news.

Ben and I walked down the street. I took him to the Wailing Wall in the heart of the old city. Together we wrote a note with healing wishes for his mother. We pushed the folded piece of paper into an opening between those large sacred stones. Thousands of others had gone before us, and the ancient wall was filled with white cemented paper. Built by longing human hands, it is part of Jerusalem; you cannot leave the city without placing in the wall a written testament of your longing.

Ben was hungry, and we set out for the McDavid's, the kosher variant of McDonald's. Ben shone with pride because, of all the children at his kindergarten, he was about to become the first who had eaten there. We bought the largest and juiciest hamburger. Our eyes met above a red plastic cup suited for giants. I looked into the wise old eyes of a five-year-old face. In him I saw the love of his mother and the wisdom of his father. At that moment I knew that I could never leave this boy.

"Do you think my Ima is going to die?"

"I don't know, sweetheart. Your mommy will always be with you, even if she is no longer alive. But Ben, it's still too early to think about the worst. Where is this question coming from?"

Ben did not have to think long for an answer. "At night a man often comes and sits on my bed. He has long hair and his eyes are different from all the eyes in the world. It's as if they are made from the moon. He says his name is Jeshua. Jeshua ben Joseph. His father's name is Joseph, and he has a brother called Judas. He is really nice and often visits me. Yesterday he stayed until I fell asleep. At first I couldn't sleep because there were very many footsteps in the hallway and many crying voices, so I didn't dare to go to the toilet or ask for some warm milk. I was scared, and then luckily Jeshua came to sit with me, and he told me a bedtime story about a world where there is no end and no beginning. He stroked my head and told me to be strong and to pray for my Ima."

"Dear Ben, have you told your parents about this?"

"I did at first, but then I did not tell them anymore. Abba said it was nonsense. I think he knows very well who Jeshua is but believes I am still too small to understand. Do you believe me?" He searched my face.

"I believe you, Ben. Truly and without a doubt."

He heaved a sigh of relief, took my hand, and asked if he could sleep in my bed. I nodded approvingly. "That's good," Ben said, "because then Jeshua can meet you, too."

We went home. I had phoned the office of the Rav, but there was no news. I showed Ben pictures of my family. He was delighted to see that at home in the Netherlands I had a dog. I told him about the windmills and the dykes, and together we painted cows. He took the bear that I had taken on my journeys since childhood and I nodded consentingly to his silent request whether he could have it.

He went weak with laughter when I confessed to him

that when I was a child, my father had tricked me into believing that chocolate milk came from brown cows and ordinary milk from white ones. Ben wanted me to tell him everything about my Ima and Abba, and I taught him the Dutch names: mamma and papa. He pronounced the words carefully, as if he understood that these sounds were precious to me. It was late before we fell asleep, and I decided to never stop loving him when I heard his young voice first wishing good night to his bear, then to Jeshua, and then to me. With a safe thumb in his mouth, curled up next to me he fell into a deep sleep. That night there was another phone call. It was Ben's father asking me to return home with Ben. The taxi would come and fetch us in half an hour. Rebecca had been brought home and she wanted to say good-bye to her children. In a daze I hung up the phone. The world stood still and I had no idea what I should tell Ben. It was not necessary, though, because at that moment I felt Ben's hand slipping into mine. He already knew. Five minutes later we were dressed and sat waiting for the taxi. Jeshua, Ben, the bear, and I.

That morning, Rebecca died in her husband's arms. She left her body behind and the wind carried her away.

Abbadia di San Giorgio, Italy, Spring 2008

The memory of Rebecca remains clear in my mind. I am nearly fifty years old now. Five years older than she ever became. At times I get a bit shaken when I meet someone in the street who resembles her or when I seem to hear her voice. It took a long time for me to let go of the thought that I should phone her or tell her something, and even three years after she passed away I found myself standing at the checkout holding a bag of her favorite cookies. I had forgotten that she was no longer there. As if a heart refuses to accept the fact that someone so precious could ever have gone. It took six winters for me to truly accept that she would never be returning.

Her Ben also became my Ben. Each month of the years that he was growing up, I wrote her a letter. I knew she was there somewhere to hear my words. Each first Sunday of the month, I posted the letter to New York. Each following Saturday, I received a card from Sarah, Rebecca's niece and Rav Abraham's new wife. She had received the letter in good order. Each year Ben and I took a plane to their new house. I understood that the daily confrontation with the old house, the street, and the area in which they had lived had become too painful for his father, and the family had moved to New York, where Sarah was waiting for him.

I am telling you this story amid the silence of a monastery. I am writing the codes in an old abbey. Between me and the wall is the church of Jeshua, and if there is no such thing as coincidence, one of the codes is written on the wall. I hope that your eyes will meet the words of the codes with joy. That they will bring you prosperity and healing in the same way that they changed my life. I should tell you that, as you and I live this book together, Rav Abraham died two months ago. His wife, Sarah, told us that he was ready to leave his life and that he longed for a new meeting with his Rebecca.

Marrying Abraham cannot have been easy for Sarah. He was a man who had been in love with his first wife all his life. The legacy of Rebecca's love was great and unforgettable. Sarah was a member of her family, and true to tradition, the first to be wed took the place of the one who had passed away. An ancient tradition, once written down by a wise man, with the intention of making certain that children would always grow up in a loving family and that women need not lose their way in the desert. In those days, a single woman with children was doomed.

The love that Sarah had for the children gave this extraordinary woman the strength to live through a one-sided marriage. As no other, she knew the importance of Rav Abraham's work. As a wise primordial mother with a heart filled with warmth and a head full of understanding, she had endless patience not only with the children and their sorrow, but also for the rows of people who daily needed advice or support from her husband. In the room next to her kitchen she taught young Jewish women about the affairs of women.

When we received Sarah's message that Rav Abraham had passed away, Ben and I took a plane as soon as possible. We joined the family in Jerusalem and together we mourned for ten days, as is customary. Just like the days when we had said good-bye to Rebecca, we sat on the floor together as tradition required.

People arrived from all corners of the world to say good-bye, and it struck me as bizarre that during a funeral the true meaning of someone's life becomes apparent. Rav

Abraham, just like his Rebecca, was loved right down to his very soul. He had been a father, friend, husband, coach, and teacher all at the same time. It had been his wish to be brought back across the ocean so that he could be laid to rest next to Rebecca.

It became a reunion and a farewell, but above all a deep silence prevailed. The final prayer for the dead, the kaddish, was read by a pastor, a rabbi, a Buddhist, and a female preacher. Everyone enjoyed it and also said it was disgraceful. Was it my imagination that I heard Abraham laugh? Even on his last day on earth he did not let the chance go by to show which garden he came from. His voice was one of unity and connection. He did not see any difference.

On the eleventh day, I received a message from the notary. He asked Ben and me to stop by. He read us a document containing all kinds of arrangements made for Ben. He had been instructed to personally give me a thick white envelope and a small box. I recognized the Rav's seal on the back of the letter. It was intact.

We thanked the notary for his good care, and while Ben went in search of future loves in the nightlife of Jerusalem, I went into the silence of the garden to read his last letter to me.

My Bubeleh,

This is my last letter to you. In the coming months we are bound to speak with each other at precious moments, but I know that my life will soon be completed. That is why you will receive this letter after I have died. It is good as it is, and I am looking forward to visiting other lives and lessons. Do not see this writing as a fare-well letter. I will never say good-bye to you.

This letter is a document of gratitude for lovingly taking in my son. Our Ben has become a wonderful human being, and I know that a challenging life is ahead of him. He has come to the earth to change things that need to be changed. An important task awaits him. The night Rebecca died, she asked me to marry you so that you would become the mother of her Benjamin. I was neither allowed nor able to do this. It is against the law for a teacher to marry his student, and although

I realize that this law was written before the days when men and women would teach each other, I made the conscious decision not to violate it. I was neither allowed nor able to ask you to be my wife.

Something different was written in the stars. Their calculations showed me that you would one day meet another love. Do not forget that stars are messengers of the universe and that within them are stored the layers of time that harbor various scenarios. Everything already is, all possibilities and outcomes are present. Each choice you make is already stored in the memory of the universe and with the scenario you choose, the ones that are not chosen fade away to different times. That is why I chose not to live the experience with you, because you and I were not made for each other as man and woman. I was your teacher and you were my student, but know that I have experienced being a student on many occasions. You and I are the same. The male and female duality of the same energy.

Ben is the Jeshua in our family. Do not forget that families also have a soul. In each family soul everyone lives their own story but also the story of the family. And in the same way as human beings, a family experiences the same duality. That is why there is as much light as darkness in the same soul. Self-hatred, misfortune, and power stand opposite love, joy, and strength. In this way, a family soul retains its balance. Every family has a Ben, a rebel, for whom the world will never be big enough and for whom wisdom can never travel too far. The rebel needs a world in which he can think and move freely, without a belief or traditions that are imposed upon him. He greatly longs for freedom because it is his duty to bring renewal.

That is what Ben is. He will not rest until he knows the secrets of the world, and this is why you, aside from his own mother, were the most suitable woman to look after him while he grew up. My knowledge has been implanted in his soul, but in you he found what he was searching for, the frequency of love, wisdom, abundance, and freedom. From the first moment that he started wiping his nose on your sleeve, I knew that you were connected by an invisible link. Freedom is your highest good. Rebecca, too, was aware of this, and that is why she passed on to you her most precious child, her Benjamin. Despite the fact that you yourself were still so young, you took him into your arms.

I have one remaining request of you. I ask you to unveil the codes. The moment has come. You will notice that, in the ensuing times, the universe will spread out the codes like raindrops from the sky. The world no longer has a choice. Once we know that we are the world, then we understand that we can heal it by healing ourselves. We then will carry our nature in love, because it is mother earth who nurtures us and lets us breathe. Then we will understand how important it is to live the codes. The codes show us the way out of confusion. Write, Bubeleh, write! Do not doubt yourself, because you may unveil the codes, and precisely because you are a woman, the soul will be felt between the words you write. It is the feminine force of the universe that connects all matter. Use the power of stories, just like all the wise women before you have done by immersing their wisdom in fairy tales and stories. Feel the Vida Cita, the inner wind, blow under your wings when you write. Write about life, about death, and everything that lies in between. Write as if your soul depends on it, and if at times you no longer know how to continue, then lay your ear in the wind and it will whisper my words to you. With this letter, I am sending you a story of my father. It was written down by my mother. I give it to you. You are a story woman just like she was, and when you read her story, you will understand why the time has come to write the codes.

Take good care of Ben. Watch over him as if he were your own child, and I will always stand by you both.

Until a later time, dear Bubeleh.

Your Abraham

I stroked the letter and wondered whether he had cried while he wrote it. He was right. I would have married him if he had asked me. Not from love for him, but from love for the fact that he was my teacher. He was the father every woman would wish for. The husband beside whom you would be proud to stand, and his mystical heart was a challenge for every woman. To me he was all of these things. But my lover he was not. At times I had smelled the fragrance of his warmth, a pleasant and spicy fragrance, and there had been moments when I wondered what kind of lover he would be. He was right. He was not my love.

You will understand, dear reader of my words, that the signal to me to write the codes felt grandiose. During our first meeting, Abraham had told me about it, and he made me promise him not to disclose the codes until he asked me to do so. This moment had now arrived and, curiously, I opened the second letter. The story by his mother. Written in neatly arranged letters with, now and then, a feminine curl.

The Story Woman

Somewhere in the world once lived a story woman. She was the guardian of all the wise stories in the world. The art of telling stories had been handed down to her, from mother to daughter and to granddaughter. It had been this way for centuries. From time immemorial. The story woman spun her wisdom in between the words. Letters made from invisible thread made the words breathe. This was who she was. A story woman. According to a story, she died on the day when people no longer wanted to hear her stories. The stories of mother earth were replaced by books and words, and even the ocean no longer knew what it should do with the lost words. They drifted ashore and slowly became the tooth of time in sandcastles. On that day, the story woman decided to die. Together with her last breath, wisdom left the world.

In the land without boundaries and without time, God already sat waiting for her. He could not wait to hear her stories, and soon it became quieter and quieter in heaven. All the ears of the universe joined in the listening. When she had told her final story, God shook his head in surprise. Why had the earth forgotten these words? He did not quite understand, because knowledge in words is only a shadow of wordless knowledge. Then, on a night that was sufficiently dark and shrouded, God slipped onto the earth. There he found thick books adorned with golden letters and thick leather jackets that talked of how the world came into being. At some point in the books he found an illustration below which was written his name. He had never seen his own face before. He read about guilt and hell, about power and darkness, about high and low, and he shed universal tears when he read about so much hunger and oppression. The world had forgotten who he was, and had written a new story clothed in a history that he did not know.

When he returned from his journey, God shook awake the story woman. "Let's get to work, there is no time to be lost. I will dig for you the deepest possible well in the universe, and each morning, aided by all angels, you will shake out the divine-code blankets. Let them rain onto the earth: as words like pearls, wisdom as keys, and desires as secrets. Ask the wind to catch them and whisper them on further. Call the sun to warm the hearts and ask love to put desires into dreams." And thus it happened. For each book that had ever been burned by history, the angels shook out the words, waiting for the wind to catch them.

The story woman wrote during the night, and the day-time task of the angels began at the well of wisdom. They shook out all story blankets carefully. Secrets were revealed, keys opened doors, and words of hope found their way downward. Somewhere on the earth, people heard invisible words being whispered that their ears could not hear but that were felt with their hearts. Their inner voices showed the way to the hidden caves where parchment documents rolled into jars had been waiting to be found. A farmer in Al-Minya in Egypt found in a limestone box a forgotten but very much alive codex. In the desert of Nag Hammadi, also in Egypt, a boy by chance discovered earthenware jars filled with handwritten letters on old rolls of parchment. Near the saltiest sea on earth, in Qumran, south of Jericho, jars were found containing the oldest story that the world for a long time had been searching for. It rained codes.

On the earth lived a wise man. Under the bedroom

of his palace was a hidden cellar. A cellar that few knew existed. There lay thousands of scrolls waiting on the shelves, carefully sorted according to age. They were lying in a faint light that would not bleach the precious scrolls. As the story went, the memory of human beings could be found there, and one night God carefully made his way into the cellar, accompanied by the story woman. They searched for the handwritten manuscript of Jeshua, who had lived a long time before. They found it and took it with them. The wise king on the earth had no intention of ever sharing these words with others. They would put his life in danger, and to be honest, it did not really matter. Because the knowledge of Jeshua could not be captured in words; it lived in stories. Words that should not be read but should be lived until the day that a new Jeshua would be born on earth.

That morning, the wise man woke up in his palace. He had had a dream about losing the key. He had forgotten about the code. Actually, God had told the angels not to laugh. Amusement was forbidden, but even God had to hide a smile when he heard the pious king mutter: *"Mein lieber Gott, wo ist der Schlüssel?"* (My dear God, where is the key?)

The Jeshua Code

The Law of Forgiveness

When you make the two into one, and when you
make the inner like the outer and the outer like
the inner, and the upper like the lower, and when
you make male and female one, so that the male
will not be male nor the female be female, when
you make an eye replace an eye, a hand in place
of a hand, a foot in place of a foot,
an image in place of an image,
then you will enter the Kingdom.

—JESUS, THE CHRIST (GOSPEL OF THOMAS)

It was the first Thursday after the mourning period. Rebecca had passed away three weeks before. Life remained life even though time had stood still for us. The Rav had informed me that he wished to continue with the lessons. The loss of his wife caused an emptiness in the house that the voices of her children could not fill. Abraham told me of his plans on the last day of mourning: He wanted to round off his affairs and move to America. He had wanted to emigrate at an earlier time, but Rebecca had asked him not to go yet. She had grown up in Bethlehem. She could not and would not leave Israel. Each week she visited Ephratha, a place not far from Bethlehem. In the cave of Machpelah, the grave of primordial mother Rachel, she said her prayers and asked for help for everyone who needed it. Rachel's grave not only was the last resting place of this mother of mothers; other venerable mothers and fathers such as Abraham and Sarah, Isaac and Rebecca, and Jacob and Leah from the five books of Moses had also left their bodies behind in this cave.

There had been more to Rebecca's weekly journey than just her prayers. Around the grave of Rachel she wound thick strings of red wool. In between the threads she braided Rachel's energy. Rachel, the mother of the world who had protected all of her children against evil. On many occasions Rebecca wrote special texts while seated on the grass, texts that her husband, Abraham, regarded in awe. She had no idea where the words came from. In large strokes she entrusted the wisdom of women to her black notebook. She had a special connection with Rachel, and in silence she talked with her. There, on the side of the road, Rachel had left life long ago when she gave birth to her youngest son. Jacob, her husband, named the child Benjamin, son of the right hand, and he buried Rachel in the cave. Rebecca named her youngest son after the son of Rachel and she, too, had had to fight for her life when she gave birth to him.

When Rebecca returned home from the hospital, a long row of people stood waiting in front of her house. Each of them wanted her to bind the red cord on them and give them a prayer. She lovingly made a bracelet of the red cord around the left arm of whoever asked, appraising them with earnest eyes while using her tongue to knot the cord seven times. The accompanying prayer contained the seven codes of life, and Rachel's energy protected the wearers of the cord against evil.

It was to become a task that I later would take over from her, at her request. But I was to take over from her a much greater task, because before her final farewell, early in the morning and an hour before she closed her eyes forever, she had taken my hand and asked me to look after her Ben. On that day, when I had hardly reached womanhood, I promised her to enfold Ben in my soul as if he were my own, and I thus became a mother without ever having borne a child. She asked me to go to Rachel's grave. There, her teacher would be waiting for me and initiate me, so that I, just like her, could become a la Que Sabe, and could take over her task of tying the red cords.

On the Thursday on which I was to be initiated in the fourth code, I traveled with Ben to his parental home. I was allowed to walk into Rav's office. His room was still empty and on his desk were stacks of letters of comfort and appreciation. He entered softly, sat down, and moved his chair directly opposite the chair on which I was sitting.

The fear I had had of him was gone and my respect for him had grown. He was the best teacher a student could hope for. He asked me about Ben, and I told him about Ben and his Jeshua.

"Abraham, who is Jeshua? And what is the connection between him and Ben?"

The Story of Jeshua

"Jeshua is the most difficult code. His story is not a simple one, and one's inner light must shine brightly in order to understand the story of his sacrifice. To some he is the rebel, to others a holy man. Jeshua carries the code of unconditional love and forgiveness. He is the visible and human expression of the first code. He is the face of unity, and this makes him the son of God.

"He was removed from our history when people wanted to divide belief into Judaism and Christianity. Originally there was no difference. The world was born with a single religion of wisdom, without a name or a face, accessible for everybody, and usable. By birth, Jeshua was a Jew. He was the son of Miriam bat Joachim and Joseph ben David. From his mother he inherited love and from his father wisdom. At an early age his mother saw how special he was, and she hid his gifts. She was a woman who knew, but she protected him until the day that she could no longer hide what had become so clearly visible. Jeshua did wondrous things. He changed water into wine, and when he laid his hands on those in pain, their suffering disappeared. The small village in which the family lived began to be fearful of the gifts of her son and, in order to protect him, his father took him to a special school. There he was taught the mysticism of life, and he lived among teachers who carefully prepared him for his task.

"Who he would become was written in the stars, and the story of his life is a testament of his gift. At an early age he married Miriam, a girl who lived next door to him and had the same name as his mother. Together they started a family, in line with Jewish tradition, but Jeshua was driven by his gifts and from far away, people came to him to be healed or comforted. One day he followed his calling and left his village so as also to become a father to the poor. He applied his spiritual gifts to teach people to live the codes of life.

"We are all One. One we are. He knew no difference in religion or background and saw in everyone the light of God.

"This Mahatma Gandhi of his day, in the old eras that had not yet been counted, used the silent weapon of peace. Peace is a powerful weapon. It is the door to everything. Unarmed, he lived his life, and each answer he gave was born from peace. Jeshua is the code of God's soul. That is his story, and in order to understand the meaning of his existence, you need an opposite, because one thing exists by the grace of another. So it happened that Jeshua, king of the poor, came to stand opposite Herod, king of the rich. The soul opposite the ego. Herod was unable to see the voice of his creator in the face of this poor man. In his palace stood a large golden statue of the sun, surrounded by fragrant candles and stimulating incense aimed at placating his Lord. Jeshua had nothing to offer except for his unconditional love. The king of the soul was willing to share his throne, but the king of the ego was not. Time provided a meeting between them in history, one that would have grave consequences.

"The story of Jeshua was rewritten by a man from history by the name of Irenaeus, Bishop of Lyons. He created a story in which there was only space for the four corners of the universe and its four universal winds. To this he linked the four gospels. All other gospels from that day on were considered heretical, and in the fire of his hatred the words of Thomas, the gospel of Judas, the letters of Paul, and the wisdom of the Egyptians were burned. He invented one single faith with one God in heaven and one king on earth. On that day, universal wisdom was banned and the different monotheistic faiths were born, because all other writings were cast away. The codes of Jeshua were banned to a secret world, and the evangelical stories serving as metaphors for the codes of life were carefully hidden by brave human hands, in jars, caves, and graves.

"Had Jeshua been predestined to die as an old man? Was it indeed his wish to die as an old man and as the founding father of his family? Time has shown us, because the choice that Jeshua made from the field of endless possibilities was to deliberately become an example of his code. Until the last day, he refused to defend himself. The king of the ego begged him to give up his peaceful resistance, and in the hidden chambers of his palace he cried bitter tears, because nailing the son of God to the cross would place the light opposite the worst darkness. Who would ever be willing to play this part?

"Had it been a coincidence that Judas, for thirty pieces of silver, had sold the place where his confidant Jeshua could be found? Who dared to betray the king of the poor? His kiss would be the way in which Judas would identify him, so that Pontius Pilate's men could lead the right man away. Only later, centuries later, when a child found the carefully hidden gospel of Judas in a cave, could a new meaning be given to the 'betrayal' by Judas. Jeshua consciously chose to die. Even Peter, who wanted to protect him from the impending danger, was chased away by Jesus. He did not want to hide, so he pushed Peter back, stepped forward, and said: 'I am the man you seek. My name is Jeshua ben Joseph from Nazareth.'

"The rest is a sad account of ego and the absence of love. On the day he died on his own cross, with his last breath his code could be heard: 'Forgive them, Father, for they know not what they are doing.'"

I was deeply moved. What had become of this love-filled rebel? I had hoped that there was somehow no truth to his story, but in all writings his history could be found. He had really lived. Abraham told me that a professor who specialized in the history of Jeshua had told him that after studying for years he still did not know who this man really was. His story was not easily understood, and his code was the highest code except for the code of God. Of all the gospels that tell his story, most were written a hundred years after his death.

Abraham explained to me that once every few years, an archangel comes to earth with a clear story. Every tradition knows at least one. Mother Teresa, the Dalai Lama, Gandhi, Martin Luther King, Jr., Nelson Mandela, all teach us to live the code of peace with civil disobedience as the only way. I asked him whether it was a coincidence that these people were often killed in the name of power. The Rav nodded: "The path of true peace makes one fearful. As much fear as there is, there is as much peace. The world must strive for peace until humanity understands Jeshua's words: 'When you make the two into one, you will become a son of man. We people are not the same, but we are equal.'"

I wondered whether the world would ever change. Whether we would ever stop killing our own children in useless wars. Whether one day we would be capable of sharing in an equal way the abundance of food that mother nature offered. Whether we would one day be willing to stop living based on power, and live based instead on the inner strength of love, harmony, calmness, peace, and happiness.

Abraham smiled: "Bubeleh, there will come a day when you will write a book and make an appeal to your readers. But be prepared that only half of them will understand you and that the other half will be malignant toward you. Do not let it make you sad, and understand that one part serves the other. This is the most important lesson that Jeshua teaches us. There are people who dare to grow and show themselves, but there are also those who choose to remain in the shadows. One is no less than the other. Each human being has a unique talent, a talent of his or her own, but besides this we all share the talent of being a human. A soccer player is famous for doing something for which others do not have the talent. This creates admiration. Spiritual teachers who teach about the art of being human do something for which everyone has the talent. Digging around in the conscience of your readers is often confrontational, because you touch on sensitive spots and hidden sorrow. The comfort you can offer them is that no one is perfect. Not you, not me, and not Jeshua either. A human experience was not made to be perfect because there will always be an opposite. Because of this opposite we can experience life. Love sees itself by the grace of hatred. But remember that we are perfect souls in a dual form. The greatest sinner has a perfect soul but a broken personality. Our intention to become a better person is the reason that by falling over and picking ourselves up again we promote our inner growth. If we want, we never stand alone. Never. There is an invisible field of love between our visible lives. We form a part of it. Always. The lesson that Jeshua teaches us is that sins are part of life and that peace is the way to love."

Abraham walked over to the bookcase, and from behind the books he took a rolled-up piece of parchment. It consisted of two containers with hand-carved handgrips, making it possible to roll the written Hebrew letters from left to right. Abraham read it with me. Where I did not understand the words, he translated them for me. When we had finished reading, there was silence between us. For a moment I did not know what to say. Finally I broke the silence: "It may sound strange, but the only way I can explain it is that I felt the words I read. As if they came to life."

Abraham nodded in agreement: "That's right, these are words translated from one of the oldest writings in the world. Sefer Yetzirah, the book of creation, is the book of Abraham written in code language. A secret language was used because the knowledge from this book was meant to be taught by word of mouth. One can hardly call it a book, because it contains only a few hundred words, in which all the codes of human existence and the universe have been noted down. The codes were put in a readable version by Rav Akiba ben Joseph. He was a loving prophet, and just like Jeshua, he died a gruesome death because of his passive resistance to those in power.

"The compounded letters from the book of Abraham are words that the mind cannot understand. The heart recognizes them, and that is how they come to life. Do not forget that the language of Jeshua is a language of images. They are words containing emotions, and in between, the letters move the meanings. These are explained differently by everyone, and that is why there are so many interpretations. But this manuscript is the purest I have ever come across. It is the book of Abraham, the book of creation. It is precious, and one day it will show itself. But not yet. On the day that religion is willing to meet spirituality, the words will want to be born."

The Jeshua Code

Together we continued reading, and right before my eyes the codes came to life.

When we look at the story of the codes, the metaphor of its history becomes visible. The first code, the God Code, teaches us that we are One. We all carry the same power inside us. We are the light. We are all a particle of a larger whole. The second code makes us remember who we are. Adam's garden is our garden, and in his earth we can and may create whatever we wish. The birthright that each of us has is the free will to make choices. We can plant fertile thoughts but also barren ones. The laws of nature do apply. Without judgment, without differentiating. Whether the seed is good or evil is not for him to decide. He sees to it that what is planted can be harvested. The third code, that of Eve, teaches us that we have a human soul and that this soul knows the secret of our lives. She knows why we are here and what we want to make visible. Each human being is born with a deep desire, and we want this desire to be fulfilled. This is the reason why we are here: the manifestation of ourselves. This is a very important fact, and at the moment a human being looks into the mirror of his soul, he makes contact with his dignity. Because who are we to be so grand? The creator allows us to. But do our surroundings, and above all ourselves, allow it? This is where human beings meet the fourth code. The Law of Forgiveness.

Jeshua is the face of forgiveness. There is no sin, no blame. There are lessons. Calling things sins make us small and unworthy. We deny our sins or we put the blame on others. We push aside our mistakes or make excuses for ourselves. We ask others to forgive us, but are we able to forgive ourselves? Do we allow ourselves to be who we want to be? When have we become good enough to allow ourselves this?

Everything begins with your own heart, and we seldom have the courage to look at our own lessons and ask ourselves for forgiveness. The lessons we live inflict wounds to the soul that others cannot heal. We must forgive ourselves. Then we can once again become whole and complete.

The code story of Jeshua is that no one is without sin: He who is without sin, cast the first stone. We live life through falling over and picking ourselves up again, and each day every human being has the possibility of saying: "I forgive myself." Put down the cross of hidden sins that you carry with you. Step out from the shadow of your ego. You are good enough, because between you and what you call God there is no difference other than the conviction that lives in your head. There is no salvation in suffering. The light of all that is is love and healing. Joy and happiness. Free yourself from the lessons that bring you darkness. Allow your heart to breathe and heal yourself. Heal your body, your heart, your unblemished soul, and in silence whisper the following words: "I am whole. That is what I am. Amen."

We were both in tears. I almost did not dare to look at Abraham. My heart pounded. I knew his questions: "What do you have to forgive yourself for? What is the reason that you do not dare to acknowledge your own light? Why are you in this country to search for yourself?"

When I had left the Netherlands I had heard myself saying to my mother: "I am going to search for myself, but I will be back." What was the reason that I had traveled so far from myself?

Then I did something that women are very good at.

I turned the question around and asked Abraham in the shadows of the evening light what he himself had to forgive himself for. My eyes told him not to ask me the question at that moment, and so as to protect me, he became the student and I the teacher.

"Rebecca should not have had any more children. The ten of them were enough, and the doctor warned us. But she was adamant that her Benjamin be born. She could not be talked out of it. I was not able to withstand her temptation, and I was startled and felt a deep sense of guilt when Benjamin announced himself. During his birth she fought for her life and claimed the name she would give him, as if she knew something that I did not. Benjamin's birth was a mission to her. The answer lies with a woman you will soon get to know."

I asked him what he had done to forgive himself. There was no blame, after all. What was the reason that he nevertheless blamed himself for a death he had no part in?

He nodded tiredly: "If I were to forgive myself, then I would love life. This is something I was not taught. I was not taught to trust in the fact that life is a safe place to live in. If I were really able to, I would be as great as I myself wanted to be and I would go where I wanted. Only then would I really live the codes."

He was right. That is how it is. Life is a great place to live in. As great as you yourself can wish for.

What Do You Have to Forgive Yourself For?
Living the Fourth Code

There is a law in this life that teaches us that forgiveness does not mean that we approve of what has happened to us. What we can do, however, is to put it where it belongs. We can carry it with us for the rest of our lives and experience the burden. We can also put it aside and know that we are not responsible for everything that happens to us, but that we can take the responsibility for how we deal with our wishes for the future. Are we daring enough to take responsibility for our lives or do we choose to remain victims of it? Dare we become the creator of our own life and our own fate?

The Miriam Code

The Law of Love

As long as the truth resides somewhere, history will not be falsified.

—ANCIENT PROVERB

I traveled to the village where Rebecca was born. The world is infinitely beautiful to eyes that wish to see. It felt as if I were traveling back in time. The driver of the bus announced my stop, and I got off. Abraham had explained to me that I should walk over the hills and that I would then see a curious-looking house. There I would find Anna, the famous la Que Sabe, Ben's grandmother, the woman who had raised Rebecca.

I walked up to the door and knocked softly. Anna opened the door, and I looked into the most piercing eyes I had ever seen in my life. She smelled of flowers and her gray hair was tied up into a thick bun. Her warm strong hands pulled me inside welcomingly and she gently stroked my face: "Your energy is like hers. You resemble Rebecca. How are the children and how is my Ben?"

She handed me a cup of tea brewed from green leaves with a strange, fresh taste, and the smell of the house gave me the feeling of having been transported to another time, just like Alice in Wonderland. Everything in her home was made of natural materials. The chairs were woven from the reeds of dry grass and the walls had been brushed down in earthy shades, but what stood out most was her garden. In the middle of this dry landscape I saw an oasis of blossoming plants. In the center of this wonderful garden stood a tree, a beautiful old tree. It had a trunk thicker than I had ever seen, with roots that seemed to grow down into the center of the earth. On the tree were hanging gleaming apples, hidden in a sea of green leaves.

Anna saw my face and nodded. She knew that I recognized the tree of my dreams. It was the tree of life with the branches of life. The tree of knowledge and wisdom. I looked at her inquiringly, and she told me that according to the story, this tree had been planted by Miriam, the mother of Jeshua, in memory of her son.

I knew Anna from Rebecca's stories. She had told me that her mother was a curandera, a healer. She knew the secrets of nature, the healing properties of herbs, and the power of prayer. She knew how to make wishes find fulfillment, and from the irises of those who visited her, she could tell what their life's purpose was. I had been prepared for a meeting with an extraordinary woman, but what she radiated went beyond my expectations. She was love. She was the face of peace.

I understood that deep experience Rebecca had gained when this house was her home. The energy of this place made searching unnecessary. Here in this house time stood still; the outside world disappeared and the heart became calm. It felt as if all that I had carried with me in my life could be put aside. I sensed the fatigue, the sorrow, and the tension of the past weeks dissipate. The journey to the codes was an intense experience for my mind, heart, and soul. Anna showed me to a large hammock in the garden. I slid into it, and swiftly fell asleep.

I dreamed that I was in the Netherlands. I was sleeping in the bed of my youth and dreamed that I was having a dream. A vividly realistic dream. In the middle of the night I woke up. My body continued to sleep, but I slipped from my bed. Something had called out to me and in front of the window hung a white rope ladder. I climbed out through the window, stepped onto the ladder, and effortlessly made my way up. The rope was soft and woolly and it seemed to be made from cloud material. I climbed past clouds on which beautiful birds lay sleeping while the stars played with the light. When I reached the last rung of the ladder, an inviting hand was stretched out to me and I was gently lifted up. I stepped into a field, a floating layer of clouds. In the middle of this field stood a man. His smooth skin was pale, but nevertheless I sensed that he was old, very old, older than anyone I had ever known. The skin of his hands felt soft; his eyes looked friendly and had a strange color—the color of the moon. He radiated a deep calmness. Uninhibitedly I walked by his side, and on our way he pointed out various shapes. I did not recognize them, but they had translucent colors. I saw colors I had never seen before and could not name them.

When I wanted to ask him if perhaps he was an angel, it was as if he had read my thoughts, and he said: "You have seen me before. You know me from when you were little and could still see your dreams. Each person knows me, because I live in the heart of love."

We were standing in front of a door. A floating white door supported by clouds. I wondered what was behind this door and looked at him questioningly. "There is someone who would like to speak with you." I was quite tempted to follow him. It had been my heart's desire to find out what things looked like on the other side, but I also knew that heaven harbors no time or memory. I wondered whether I would still be able to remember myself once I had passed through the door. How would I find the way back? I asked him whether the people who passed through the door actually returned. He told me that this seldom was the case. Very seldom. Never, in fact. On some occasions people could see the door, but their time had not yet come. In such cases they were lovingly put back on earth.

He opened the door and took my hand. I wanted to go with him, yet I did not really dare to. I was very much afraid that I would no longer be able to remember myself. What should I do? At that same moment, I decided to leave my heart outside the door. I carefully hid it under the threshold. Now I would always be able to find my way back because my heart would perpetually long for me.

The door opened and I tumbled into a world without time. My eyes needed to adjust to the light. I was slowly lifted up and I heard music that my ears could not hear. There was no longer any difference between hearing, feeling, seeing, and knowing. Everything was One. Everything was love and yet not. There was no difference between something and nothing. It could better be described as blissful harmony, a quiet, fulfilling feeling. I asked him if

I now was dead, and he nodded: "In your mind you are dead, but to your heart you are alive. You are home.

"Someone is waiting for you with a message. She has been asked to teach you a code. The code of love. She is the story woman. She is the one who has made your dream so that she would speak with you." At that same moment I saw her and looked into the face of the dream maker. I had seen her before in my dreams. She might well be Rebecca's grandmother. She had exactly the same eyes.

"Bubeleh, I have had you brought here because I need to teach you a code. You cannot live life without having an understanding of death. You cannot embrace life if you are afraid to die. In the world of time there is a beginning and an end, but in the world where your soul lives there is no such measure. The code of death in fact is a new beginning, a new creation. It is part of life, and those who have died are not gone but have traveled on to other times and new lessons. You can talk to them by sending your thoughts to them. They answer you. Not in words such as you are familiar with, but instead they use life to transfer messages. The soul knows that death does not exist, but for the ego it is difficult to grasp because it is attached to all that is visible. That which is not visible does not exist to the ego. The ego is not fond of letting go, and would like everything to remain as it is. That is why the ego experiences sorrow at saying farewell. But the law of life determines that people live on from old to new layers. It is important for you to understand that also in your other lives you sow as you now do on earth. It is the same principle. The way you see life is the way it will turn out to be. This applies to all lives: those of the future, at the current time, and of the past.

"On earth you learn to create with a place and a time. The senses are the instruments that make your experiences tangible. Only when the ego can smell, taste, hear, see, or feel an object is it able to discern an object. Every palpable subject that the ego discovers is bound by time and place. It has a beginning and an end. It has a place that is close by or far away. Without place or time it is not sensed by the ego. But if something cannot be seen by the ego, it does not mean that it does not exist. Everything already is. Nothing needs to still be made, and with the power of your thoughts you make visible what before was hidden. With the power of your thoughts you attract energy to yourself by what you think and feel. You do this consciously and unconsciously. That is why it is so important not to fear sickness or death. The more you consciously surround yourself with loving thoughts, the more you attune to love. Love meets love when you think it, feel it, and are it.

"Between that which you ponder within yourself and that which is visible in your life is the concept of time. Thanks to time, you see the result grow. Therefore you can learn how to create. You plant a thought in a field of energy, and in due time it will grow and you will be able to see it in your life. The ego sees it and will have an opinion about it. It is either accepted or not. But the ego often forgets what was once planted, especially if that which is visible is the result of fearful or hidden thoughts. Plant with your feeling instead of with your thinking. Ask your heart what it really needs. The ego will answer you in forms and matter, but know that behind each object there lives a feeling, and often the ego puts a picture on the feeling that it already recognizes. But the heart has a will of its own and wants the fulfillment of its desires. That is why forms and matter provide a short-lived fulfillment, unless they are a true reflection of the heart's wishes.

"Consequently, it is important to plant based on your feelings and to trust that nature will find the best way to fulfill your desires. Sometimes the ego is so involved in battling the heart that it cannot find fulfillment and has to search continually.

"It is an art to learn to make conscious use of your thoughts and to learn to steer what you feel. You cannot stop thinking. The ego continuously thinks, and everything it thinks has two voices, a positive and encouraging voice and a negative voice of warning. One exists by the grace of the other. But your intuitive feeling is aware of the difference and knows the direction. Be true to your intuitions and let thinking do its work. Thinking considers the pros and the cons, but feeling knows instinctively. If you steer with your feeling and remain true to your desires, you will notice that your thoughts will start moving the same way.

"You live so as to practice, in preparation for later when you travel to a new dimension. There is no time here. There is only this moment. There is no later and no soon. Everything is now. We do not have the concept of time to practice with. That which we feel is immediately picked up by our thinking, which then transmits it. At that same moment, we see our thoughts appearing on the screen of our experience.

"See the earth as an exercise school. The experience

you refer to as life is a preparation for mastery. There will come a day when you will be able to see your thoughts directly on your screen of life. That is why you go through practice on earth before you come here. If you live with a fear of death, then that is what you live. If you live with a love of life, then that is what you breathe. Love life because it is too beautiful not to live. Life is the story of who you are. And . . . when at some point you are ready to let go of this life, then look back and see what you have yet to learn in your next experience. Once, when I still lived on the earth, and my stories were listened to, I told people about death. It gave them strength and courage to know that there is no final farewell. But when books appeared written by the ego, death was born and with it the fear of life. Lay your hands on life, look at the plenty it has to offer you, and see all the possibilities there are. Teach yourself and the people around you to love life. Share what you have got and who you are. Touch the people around you with all the warmth and love that you possess so that you can awaken the best in them, and make of yourself the most wonderful individual you can be. This is what life is meant for. Live in it and love it."

When she had finished talking, I felt myself being

lifted up and I descended through layers of colors. In a flash, I was standing in front of the window of my bedroom. Suddenly I remembered that I had left my heart at the door, and in panic I called out that I needed to go back because my heart was still under the threshold, but the man had already disappeared into the clouds. I had lost my heart. How was I to live?

Then I remembered the words of the story woman: "You are there where you think you are." I focused my attention on my heart and felt its longing. This feeling was picked up by my thoughts and I decided to make conscious use of my thoughts and steer them toward where I wanted to be. In my thoughts I flew through the clouds and the colored layers of time, back to the place where I had left my heart. In the distance of my imagination I saw the white door appear. When I looked under the threshold, I had the shock of my life. My heart was gone! I searched left and right in case it might have rolled away, but my heart was nowhere to be found. I was overcome with fear that it had been trampled on or that someone had taken it. At that moment I felt a hand on my shoulder. It was Rebecca. She gave me a kiss and handed me my heart. Softly she pushed me back to where I had come from and whispered into my ear: "Your heart has been purified, and everything you were not able to forget has been forgiven. Continue your life and make it as remarkable as you can."

I was woken by Anna, offering me a cup of spicy herbal tea. I wanted to tell her about my strange dream, but she told me to get going because the day was coming to an end.

It was Friday, and the sunset would herald in the Sabbath until dusk came once more on Saturday. The table had been set and within the hearth a bright fire burned. Anna beckoned me into a room behind the house that had white tiles and a square bath sitting in the ground. I realized that I must undress. She asked me when I had last menstruated and together we counted the twelfth day. She cut my nails, gently combed my hair, and examined my body. When she decided that all was pure, she led me to the bath. Step by step I descended into the water. In the middle of the bath she gestured to me to pull up my legs as if I were a baby in a fetal position. Free from the sides and the bottom of the bath, I floated with my head submerged in water. I realized that I was being initiated. At that moment she admitted me into the code of love by softly saying a prayer.

My soul felt like new and my heart was purified. Since that time, love has never again left my life.

We dined together in the warm room, on delicious crisp bread. With the bread we savored sweetly spiced meat from a large wooden bowl in the center of the table. I was to live with her for five days. We passed the days in learning, and one by one she imprinted the stories of life onto my heart. She told me about the oldest pact between women, the secrets of motherhood. She showed me Ben's life path and soothed my concerns about being too inexperienced to raise him. She gave me wise advice, and in the nighttime hours she taught me how to read the stars, how to understand the fragrance of the wind and the power of light. She taught me prayers and sounds that could heal, and the art of plants and herbs. But above all she passed on to me who she was, the greatest gift: unconditional love that would continue to surround me like a soft cloud.

On the last day of my visit, she took me to the tree. She told me that it had been grown from the seed of the oldest tree of life in the universe, with roots that touched down to the foundation of the earth. Its branches carried its fruits like sapphires. In its trunk was hidden the knowledge of the world. Anna told me to put my hands on the tree, and with my cheek touching its bark I could feel it breathe. There I stood, unaware of time, moved by its breath, and finally there no longer was a difference between the tree and myself, and I could feel its wisdom.

Anna asked me if I had a wish, and in my hands she put a mustard seed. I knew the story of Jeshua, who had used the mustard seed as an example to illustrate that from the smallest seed the grandest thing could be born. To me it was a great gift to be able to plant my desire in this garden. Just like Adam, the gardener in the second code had taught me, and with the power of my imagination, I filled the seed with my greatest wish and planted it into the fertile soil of Anna's oasis.

I was grateful to be alive, and I knew that everything I might need would automatically come my way. The days with Anna had strengthened me. She was a wonderful teacher, and when I thanked her, she regarded me with her knowing eyes. "Life will send you many teachers still. Some of them will teach you how not to live life. Others will teach you strength or perseverance and dedication. You know what is right for you. Be true to yourself. Be true to your feeling. You are the only one who knows which way you should go. Even in moments of doubt, it is better to live your own lesson than someone else's. The secret of life is that we are each other's teachers. An important task awaits you. At home Ben is waiting for you. Raise him with the codes. Teach him the laws of nature and allow him to grow like a tree with firm roots as his foundation. Water his heart with your love, and teach him the power of passion and rapture. Grant him the freedom to grow, and he will instinctively grow toward the life that best suits him.

"Travel back to the world and tell your stories. Stories in which people who heal and give warmth can live, and who give and embrace love. If you no longer know which way to go, then use your strength and ask. Focus your attention on the code of love and it will be at your side. We story women come from a lineage of the oldest women in the world. The knowledge we possess has carefully been passed down to us. Our genealogical tree reaches right back to Rachel, the mother of the world, and to Miriam and the Code of Love. If you ask her, she will always advise you, and at all times you can ask for her energy to stand by you. She will watch over you and protect you."

The Miriam Code

At a young age Miriam already knew that she would be mother to a son who held more light than many others. Miriam bat Joachim was carefully raised and initiated by her mother, Anna. At a young age she was taught the mysticism of life. She was beautiful and intelligent. When she was twelve years old, she married her neighbor Joseph, from the house of David. One day the angel Gabriel passed on a message to her telling her that she was to bear a child whom she would name Jeshua. When she was expecting her son, she and her husband undertook a great journey with only an old mule by their side. They traveled eighty miles through the desert to Bethlehem. In a stable her contractions started, and in the garden of life Jeshua cried his first breath. His mother took him into her arms and filled his soul with love, strength, and deep faith. The link between mother and son, older than the world itself, remained constantly with them. They belonged together, until the end of time.

His sandak, Simeon, who had been asked to be his god-father, expressed a prophecy that this child was to shake up the earth, and the news went through the town that a new king had been born. The astrologers had predicted his coming, and anxiously Miriam sensed that the king of the land, Herod, was overcome by fear. He gave the order to banish all local boys under the age of two from the face of the earth. That night, Jeshua's father had a dream that held a warning. Miriam wrapped her child in a cloth held to her breast, and together with her husband walked through the warm fields to Egypt. Years later the family returned to Nazareth with four sons and two daughters. And until the day that the world had become too small for Jeshua, she took care of him with all her indomitable love. She taught him the secret of her code. She told him to sit down in the grass and bring his attention to his heart.

"What is the love of your life?" she asked him. He knew what he wanted. She stroked his young cheek. "Wherever you are, whatever you need, close your eyes and feel that what you need is already present in your heart. You must know that the power of prayer does not provide the right words and does not ask the right questions. It is the power of love that sets your desire into motion. It is the power of your feeling with which you determine what you wish to see in life. When you are able to experience this feeling as if it is already there, then it will appear. Such is the law of life. I know that it is not easy to understand, but dear Jeshua, everything already exists. Observing life, hearing its sounds, appreciating its beauty, is the reason why you feel wonder in your heart. In your imagination you travel to that which your heart longs for, and this longing will allow you to experience it as if it is already there. This is how gratitude is born. When the angels hear someone's gratitude coming from the earth, then the only thing they can do is to fulfill a wish." So they sat together, mother and child, and neither of them realized how special they were.

Miriam's children grew up and went their own ways, and on the day that her husband left his life, she decided to follow her eldest son. His brothers were with him, and she knew that his days were difficult and long. She watched over him in the shadows, and on the most difficult and burdensome day she knelt by his side. She held back her tears until he died. With gratitude she received his last request to her, to adopt his youngest disciple, Johanan. He looked down at her, and in his eyes she could see that he had not suffered. In his heart he was already in the light. The angels had answered his wish.

When evening came, he was lifted from his cross and

laid into his mother's arms. She held him in her arms, just like on the first day when she had given him her eternal love. This is how the world would remember her. Her unconditional tenderness for her child.

"What is the love of your life?" Anna asked me. "The codes," I mumbled. "The codes. It is my love to understand life. Perhaps it is God I am searching for. Perhaps I am hoping to one day discover why I am here. According to Abraham, each human being consciously chooses what to experience in their life. We choose the parents we want to be born from to receive from them the personality we need for our selected experience."

There were moments when my mind was running over with questions. Because what about the hunger and poverty in this world? Or children who die too young? What was the reason that there were people who seemed to be born into luck, while many other people suffered? The rebel in me awakened and my thoughts stormed. Would I ever be able to live the codes? Anna looked at me mindfully.

"Everyone lives the codes. Deep in our heart we know that we are One. That we have a right to live. That we may be what we wish to be. We know that we are equal, even though we do things differently, and know that these colors and diversity are what makes life so beautiful. We are who we are. We need not be perfect to find the fulfillment of all our desires. We must learn to love ourselves. This is the code we must come to understand. We can immerse the world in love if we learn to love ourselves, and this is something we are not taught. We are taught to love an outer world and wait patiently for our share to come our way. It is none other than the rebel who dares to open these doors that otherwise would remain closed. It is none other than the anarchist who strives to overturn existing untruths and will not accept a fate that is imposed upon him by the makers of power. Do not be ashamed to ask your questions. Ask them out loud. Search for the answers and try to find justice where there is injustice.

"We live in a world in which children are dying. Not every soul chooses to be here for a long time. Painful as it may be, there are parents who, just like Miriam, must take their children into their arms in the knowledge that they were not able to save them. But know that her legacy whispers across the world: 'Nothing is gone until you think it is gone.'"

The next morning someone came to fetch me. A man

in a long black coat was standing at the door. On his head he wore a large hat trimmed with fur. I went on my way in search of the disclosure of the sixth code.

There were moments when I hoped that the next code would be disclosed by a gorgeous dark-haired man on a motorcycle, and that I could ride pillion in my jeans, wearing my beloved white sneakers and with my hair flowing. I knew that I could plant this choice, but oh well, leave it for what it is, I would rather follow my love. I kissed Anna good-bye, and in my bag I carried a pouch containing earth and the mustard seed.

What Is the Love of Your Life?
Living the Fifth Code

The fifth code is the Code of Love for Yourself. How light has your heart become? Have you left behind everything that your heart no longer wants to carry? Who do you want to be? What do you want to do, and how long will you put off doing this? How grand do you want to be, and what do you want to start doing? Have you given yourself permission? Are you entitled to live the life you wish for? And if so, who are you then?

Imagine standing in front of the mirror of life, and with your index finger point to yourself: "Look, that's me! This is precisely who and what I want to be!" Now what do you see?

The Moses Code

The Law of Trust

The children of Israel must call to mind the favor bestowed upon them by God and fulfill his covenant. Then God will be true to them.

—KORAN, SURA 2:40

It was hot in the car, it was a long journey, and I wished I could have stayed with Anna. The rest had done me good, and she had given me new wings. I had no idea where I was being taken, and when I asked my guide about our destination, he mumbled something I could not hear. On a sign alongside the road, I could see that we were heading in the direction of Dahab. For hours we drove through the desert, and this confirmed my suspicion that we were traveling south. My guide handed me bread and water. Many times I tried to start a conversation with him, but he remained taciturn. He put a finger to his lips as a sign that he did not appreciate it when I talked. The voice of my ego became louder and I began to get worried. Did Anna really know where he was taking me? I tried to calm myself by breathing toward my heart, but my worry increased when I saw signs loom up that showed that we were coming to the Egyptian border. At the side of the desert road stood a large advertising billboard. Beneath the dust I made out the words of a travel agency's poster: "Welcome to Tabah.

Trust is the way." Tabah is the border town between Israel and Egypt. Just in front of the border we stopped, and my guide gestured that I should take my bag and walk through the border checkpoint. Before I knew it, the car drove off. Now I really was in a panic because there I stood: a young woman, alone in the desert, in a landscape full of unfamiliar people. I searched around me for a bus stop and heaved a sigh of relief. I had enough money on me to buy a bus ticket. I was tired from the long, hot journey and wanted to return to the coolness of Jerusalem. There was nothing for me in Egypt, and the last thing I wanted was someone waiting for me at the border. I wanted to return home.

I looked at the border crossing. I saw camels and overloaded cars, crying children, cursing fathers, and exhausted mothers. There were crowds of hot and dusty people. I headed for the bus stop. I examined the timetable and found that the next bus would be leaving in two hours. I began to relax, and seated on my bag I watched the rest of the spectacle.

Just in front of the border crossing stood a man. He was wearing jeans, white sneakers, and a white shirt and was looking at me closely. I no longer knew the art of flirting, and dressed as I was, in my skirt and long-sleeved blouse, I could not understand why he was looking at me. When I looked the other way and made it clear that I was not interested in a flirting bout with an Egyptian hippie, to my great disdain he began to whistle. I once again ignored him. He then began to wave at me, and the long row of people at the border crossing began to interfere. "Hey, Gingi, *nououu, boi le kan."* "Hey, Redhead, come here!" I gave him an angry look; he was hailing me as if I were a red-haired dog. Meanwhile he began to signal to the people on my side of the border that he wanted to ask me something. In four languages it was pointed out to me that a gentleman was trying to attract my attention! Meanwhile, he had joined the long line on the other side of the road. I noticed that there were two lines: a long row made up of Israelis and Egyptians and a short row in which stood a number of tourists who seemed uncomfortably out of place. Apparently this was not the holiday season. My eyes were once again drawn to the advertising board: "Trust is the way." The customs man motioned to me to proceed. The Egyptian hippie walked over to me immediately, extended his hand, and introduced himself as David. Right away I recognized his eyes. He was Abraham's youngest brother.

I recognized his face from the picture standing on the

Rav's desk. When he talked about his brothers, he always looked at the picture and lovingly moved his hand over the frame. David grinned from ear to ear; he looked happy to see me. For my part, I was pleased to continue the journey in an air-conditioned car.

David told me that we would spend two days in a hotel at a nearby beach, because I was not expected at my next destination in the village of Milga until Saturday evening. In this place, centuries ago, the Catherine Monastery was built on Djebel Musa—the name Muslims had lovingly given to the mountain of Moses. I was familiar with the monastery because it was the place where the handwritten Codex Sinaiticus was originally kept, the Greek Bible containing the complete version of both testaments, including the Letter of Barnabas and parts of *The Shepherd of Hermas*. It was on that mountain that Moses had encountered the burning bush. At the end of the second day I was to visit my teacher in the monastery.

David dropped me off at the hotel, promising to be back in an hour so that we could share a meal. He was looking forward to hearing the latest news about his family. He had been on a repeat mission in the army when

Rebecca died. He was planning to visit the family in two weeks' time.

I enjoyed the sea breeze. It was wonderful to see people sitting at the outdoor cafés, happily having a drink. It was overwhelming to watch the sea, where many hundreds of children were splashing. It was relaxing to simply be young again for a while. I pulled the elastic band from my hair, rolled up my sleeves, changed money at the hotel's reception, and ordered a glass of cola. I was given the key to my room. On the bed in my room lay a bag. It contained an envelope with pink notepaper inside. The note had been written by Ben's eldest sister:

Dear Bub,

Don't worry. We're fine. Ben misses you and so do we. You are on your way to the sixth code, and I hope that you realize how proud we are of you. Together, the codes make up a profound path, and I sense that following the path is costing you a great deal of strength. Abba, thankfully, is home a lot, because the house is empty and quiet without Ima. On Sunday, grandmother Safta Anna is coming to spend some time with

us. We are looking forward to her visit and are curious
to hear her stories about you.

Abba asked me to pack a bag for you. He explained
that on your journey through the codes you will not get
a new teacher until the former one has let you go. The
fact that you are now reading my words means that you
have succeeded in the fifth code and are on your way to
the sixth. I imagine you will have brought a bag with
warm clothes. I have no idea what you usually wear
and so I asked for advice from the daughter of the coffee shop owner around the corner. Abba said she could
help me find the right clothes. What fun! His daughter
came with me and I was surprised at all the things she
selected. The clothes certainly are different from the
skirts and sweaters from Yentl's boutique on the corner!
The girls and I enjoyed packing your bag.

We have endured another drama involving Ben's
bear. The bear's leg was caught between the doors of
the bus, and Ben screamed blue murder as if it were his
own leg. Luckily the driver stopped, and together with
an inconsolable Ben we gathered up what remained of
the leg. In the evening Abba took the bear to the doll
mender and she sewed the leg back on. Now Ben and

his bear have been limping around for days, and we are frequently asked to kiss the bandages.

Ben told me to tell you that the envelope of this letter contains the biggest kiss in the world.

Much love from us to Uncle David. We are thinking about you, and we are with you in our thoughts.

Eve

I sniffed the letter, and the fragrance of love filled my head. I pulled back the zipper of the bag. On top was a pair of bleached jeans of a fabulous brand, a black belt, four white T-shirts, a bikini, a bottle of nail polish, mascara, a bottle of perfume, deodorant and . . . a pair of white sneakers. What luxury, what abundance! I began hopping through the room like a kangaroo. I rushed into the shower, washed my hair, and used so much deodorant that there would be no perspiring in the coming months. I had not expected that it would feel so strange to wear a pair of jeans and a T-shirt again. It felt as if I were breaking a clothing law, and for a moment I considered putting my long skirt back on. I looked at myself in the mirror. "Hello, Holland," I said to myself. "Hello, youth, hello, love for life, hello, fun, hello, me!" I could not keep away from the shoes, so with red-painted toenails I slipped into the white sneakers. The words of the dream woman came back to me: "Life is too beautiful not to live."

It was time to meet David, and I walked over to the dressing table to get my room key. There on the top lay a brochure: "Travel with us, trust is the way." This time I took good notice of the words. Third time lucky. Life speaks back to you, always. It talks to you through meetings, situations, coincidences, and I began to suspect that the sixth code would be the code of trust. But not just now. I had a day and a half left to play with the sand, the sea, and the sun. I was looking forward to life. I pulled the door shut behind me and walked into the corridor. I had the heart of a child, the body of a young woman, and the soul of . . . Well, what is a soul actually? Then I heard the story woman whisper into my ear: "A soul is the breath of God."

On Saturday, David took me to the monastery. When we said our good-byes, he handed me a letter with a request to pass it on to the Pappas of the monastery. I recognized the red seal of Rav Abraham. Upon entering, I was shown the way by a woman with long black hair. She spoke English with a thick Greek accent. She was to bring me to the Pappas. Intrigued, I walked down a long hallway filled with rare icons. In this place the codes of Adam, Eve, Jeshua, and Miriam came to life.

In the courtyard of the monastery I was introduced to a man. He was dressed in black, and on his habit hung a cross of a shape I was not familiar with. He noticed my interest in it and explained that he belonged to the Greek Orthodox Church. I gave him the letter and could tell by his face that, just like I had, he recognized the seal. His English was impeccable, though he spoke with a Greek accent. He asked me whether I had been baptized. I told him that I was not a Catholic but that I had been inside a mikvah, a holy bath. Silently I thanked Anna for the bath ritual. She, la Que Sabe, had carefully prepared me without me realizing it. He then asked whether someone had taken my confession and whether there was peace inside me. To those questions I could also give an affirmative answer, and I thanked Rebecca in silence. He took me to my cell, a small and sober room with a beautiful figurine of Miriam on the wall. He told me that I would be fetched at three o'clock, instructed me to dress warmly in clothing

that covered my arms and legs, and then asked my shoe
size before taking his leave. A few minutes later there was
a knock on the wooden door of my cell. The raven-haired
Greek lady stood there with a pot of tea, a cup of warm,
spicy soup, and a pair of climbing boots. She explained
to me that she would come back to wake me at half past
two. I slept on a wooden bed with a view of the statue of
Miriam. She was so beautiful, and I drowned in her sad,
wise eyes. No matter which church I had entered, wherever in the world I was, I could not keep myself from sitting near her for a moment to burn a candle. I had been
raised without religion or tradition, but nevertheless I visited her even in my childhood years. She was my hope and
my comfort whenever I came across her image. I always
wanted to say hello to her as if tuning my radio to her frequency. Was it my imagination that I felt my heart fill with
love? Was it my imagination that I could feel her strength?
I thought of Ben and his Jeshua. I missed him, and in my
thoughts I gave him the biggest kiss in the world. I closed
my eyes, brought my attention to my heart, and very softly
called out her name: "Hello, dear mother of all mothers.
I so hope that you are enveloped in love." I luxuriated in

the peace around me and fell asleep. I was home without being at home.

At half past two I was roused, and at three o'clock I stood dressed and waiting at the exit. The monastery stood at the foot of Djebel Musa, the mountain of Moses. We climbed up Moses' mountain under a sea of stars wrapped in the coldness of the night and the infinity of the sky. While we walked, the Pappas in his calm voice told me the Code of Moses.

The Moses Code

"The story of Moses stands for the ability of humans to perform miracles when the seed of trust lives in their hearts. The Code of Moses is about the trust that exists among an individual, his creation, and the creator. The life journey of Moses stands for the spiritual journey that each human being makes. One by one he discloses the codes during his lifetime. On the mountain where we are now walking, God spoke to Moses and gave him the codes. God told Moses to go down the mountain, back to his people, and teach the codes. Not an easy task, because on his way he got to know the good and the evil in people. On the day that his faith in the goodness of his fellow man began to waver, in his anger he broke the codes into pieces. He learned that the codes would not come to life, because they were written on stone; they could live only when they were experienced by the heart.

"Time healed his faith, and Moses began his journey. He went in search of the promised land. He walked over the bottom of the sea. He opened the water by giving voice to the code of trust and thereby left behind his inner enemies. They were washed away by the water of doubt, while he made the choice to continue walking. He chose to live from unity, love, and truth, and with his brother at his side, he walked the path of his desire. He listened while his brother Aaron spoke. Moses knew that he would never enter the promised land. He saw it lying in the distance and found his resting place on Mount Nebo, overlooking the Dead Sea. He did not need the view, because, as no other, he already knew that the promised land lived in everybody and could be found through insight. His journey was long and heavy but nonetheless promising. At the end of the inner journey, Moses had become a man who was able to show the best of himself. He dared to be big and, in his modesty, sit next to his creator. He spoke to everyone and used the name that God had given to all people in the world: 'Children of Israel, those who wrestle with God.' Israel did not represent a place or a time, but stood for all people who were in search of God within themselves.

"Moses understood the name that God had given to man, and that it referred to the struggle within themselves that they should give up. They would find the promised land in themselves by journeying with the codes. On the mountain of God, Moses indicated with his stick where his people should go, and spoke: 'Look, children of Israel, follow the path to who you are. In your memory write down who you wish to be and breathe the name of the Light in all you do. Within the breath of your life place the human that you want to be so that you know which way you need to go. Keep on until the time that, with your inner eye, you see what you wish to be with your mind, heart, and soul. Then point your index finger and show the direction you want to go: 'I am, That, I am.'

"The gift that Moses is showing us is the ability to understand. He covered his face with cloths, so that the view of the outside world would not disturb him. He knew the art of listening in silence. Reading words and under-standing them does not mean that you understand the meaning of them. What you see gets its meaning by the interpretation you give to it. The insight determines how you see it. A loving person meets love. An angry person meets hatred.

"Once a human being restores their relationship with life and its magic, they discover that all that a heart longs for already exists. The secret code is that human beings are not their desires, but rather, that it is the other way around. A human being is the visible expression of a desire. It is a law of life, and this is what Moses is showing us.

"In the universe lived a desire to make visible the code of trust, and somewhere in the world lived a man who could listen and who caught the words of trust. This is the story of Moses. In the universe live many differ-ent desires that are in search of people who will live them. This is how the desire for trust found Moses. It whispered wisdom into him and led him to the path of unity. In the silence and with the force of the mountain, unity chose to show herself. She asked him to cover his eyes so that her light—too powerful for a human to see—would not harm him. He could be rendered blind by it. She asked him not to speak, so that between his thoughts she could plant. It is said that Moses stuttered, but it is more likely that he spoke in visible and nonvisible words. The visible words were heard through sound. The nonvisible words were understood with the heart. The five books containing the history of the world that Moses was to receive held the codes for life. It was Moses' task to show people that they were in control, and could desire what they wished for, and that they could have trust in this. All that was, all that is, all that will ever be from the beginning to the end of time, is written in this Old Testament. Written in codes, from the first until the last letter, composed of a series of letters arranged with equal distance. Originally it had been written in one single, continuous, long sentence. That is how it should have remained, because that is how it was written.

"Moses learned that a life has a beginning and an end. Life is a single long sentence with a visible life and invisible life codes. From mountain to mountain, each human being moves through life. From Horeb to Nebo. From God to God. On the mountain, Moses learned that there was no difference between within and without, above and below. On the blessed day that he truly understood who he was, both visibly and invisibly, he saw how infinitely great he was. He fell to his knees in awe and spoke: "I am all and all is me. I am God and God is within me. Heed these words, Israel; God is One and One is God." On that day his ego died, and for a long time he continued to live in enlightenment."

The stones crunched under our feet. We had climbed high, very high. In this place my special travel guide built a large campfire and left me behind. "Tomorrow I will return."

The world was large under the stars, and I decided to let trust awaken in me. I chose to trust in the feeling of safety and security. I traveled back to my youth to find this sensation and bring it back to the present moment. I asked myself how many people are brought up with the knowledge that a safe place is there for them in this world, a place in which they are wanted; that they have a life in which they can be as great and as beautiful as they desire. Life is good if you want to live in it. It is peaceful if inside yourself you feel safe enough to have faith in it. Here on the mountain of Moses I made the pledge that I would never again mistrust life.

I closed my eyes and instructed my ears to watch over me. I did not want to be surprised by an animal in the night. I brought my attention to my heart. I breathed calmly and deeply a few times. I thought about Ben and felt my heart open. I felt the connection with the space that surrounded me, and after a while there was no longer an outside or an inside. I was taken up in silence, with the deep trust that life would take care of me.

Someone sat down beside me. I sensed that it was an old and wise person. I regarded the being and noticed that it was a man I did not know. He exuded warmth, and his eyes had the color of the moon. I asked for his name, and he answered that his name was Ben. Ben from the house of David. I told him that my adopted son had the same name. He took my hand and said: "I *am* your Ben." I was confused because Ben was young and this Ben was old. "Michal, I am Ben's soul. The Ben you know is a part of the soul from which we descend. Ben descends from a long line of teachers who teach the mystical knowledge of the world and pass it down from father to son. We can be found throughout history. In all beliefs and religions. Old and young. From Adam to Jeshua, from Leonardo to Benjamin."

I was surprised that he knew my name. The family in Israel had given me the name Bubeleh, that which is sweet. In the Netherlands I had my own name, and the man next to me had used my official Jewish name: Michal bat Abraham, a name that was only used on the ceremonial days of life.

I asked him where he was from. "I am from another field of time. A frequency that your physical eyes cannot see. Once you let go of life, you will be able to see me. Right now you see me with your imagination. With your eyes you cannot see me because I do not live in your world. When you travel to other times, you will find me.

"If you have any questions, then ask me now."

"Is Abraham also part of your family?"

"Abraham is the descendent of the same family soul. Just like David. He will be your husband this year, if you so choose. Ben is the youngest in the line of teachers, until your youngest son is born. You will name him Michael ben David, guardian of life."

"Is Rebecca family of mine?"

"You descend from the line of women who know the stories of the world. You descend from the line of Eve to Rachel, from Ruth to Anna and onward, from the house of Abraham."

"How many people form part of this family soul?"

"Innumerable."

Suddenly much became clear to me. I understood the recognition I had felt with Anna, Rebecca, and her daughters. It was a tremendous relief to know that Ben and I were related, from time immemorial. I felt myself filled with trust, confident at last that I would be able to raise him adequately. I was not alone. I had a field of wise old women for support. The sage soul next to me broke the silence.

"What would you like to know about life? What is the most important question in your life?"

Thousands of questions raced through my head. Which was the most important? Feverishly I thought about it. I found it in the cellar of my memory.

"How do I become all that I desire?"

"By being it."

"How do I do that?"

"Ask yourself what it would feel like if your wish came true. Plant this feeling in your heart, hold it close to you, and it will begin to live within you. At first in your inner world, and then in the outer.

"Michal, what do you want to be?"

"I would like to be the face of abundance. An abundance of wisdom, love, peace, and freedom."

"So everything, in fact?"

"Actually, yes. Is that allowed? May we wish for everything?"

"Each person has his own desires. That is why there are so many possibilities. The desire determines the frequency, what it tunes in to. Not all of us desire the same, and an endless supply is available so as to fulfill all desires. You may desire everything, because the more a human being has, the more he is able to share. It is a law of life that you cannot share if you have nothing. Share your words, your love, your feeling, your light, your talents, and, if necessary, your possessions. Share that which you can spare."

"How do you learn to have faith in the codes?"

"Everything begins with yourself. Your foundation is the faith you have in yourself. You can teach yourself the art of trusting by looking for the frequency of trust. This feeling is stored somewhere in your memory. Consciously bring this feeling into your heart. Tell yourself that you are One with everything. You are part of a greater whole. All the qualities of the greater whole are present in you. This is a law, and there are no exceptions. You already are everything, and the extent to which you have faith in this is the reason that your inner convictions shine out. Practice this, develop your capacity of imagination, and sit daily with yourself in silence."

"What about the code of death?"

"There is no such thing as death, as you already know, only a new beginning. Your mind only knows the concept of death if you are not willing to continue your growth."

"And the code of healing?"

"Everything is whole, even in case of illness. The soul is whole. The body can be ill. In such a case it is important to remember that you can have an illness, but that you yourself are not ill. With the right care a body can heal, unless the soul decides to travel on. This is difficult for the ego and the mind, but the soul knows that life is a temporary experience, with a beginning and an end. Not an easy lesson, and many a time we are moved to tears when we see the sorrow of those who stay behind. Celebrate life, Michal. It is the best way to heal."

"And the code of evil?"

"Know that everything is born from the light, from unity. You can choose to live from that foundation. To live from the light in you. The more you understand the codes, the more light you will receive. A face that looks at the darkness will become the shadow.

"Teach yourself to live in the light. The day people understand that, just like Jeshua, they can live in the light. Christ is born in each human being. All people are equal to Jeshua. That is his code. Jeshua was not divine. He was a man, with love and sorrow. He was a loving rebel and living proof that life is not made up of perfection but of the willingness to live. At the end of the inner journey of the codes, the initiation into the light is waiting."

"Ben from the house of David. Who am I?"

"Moses asked God: Who are you? God answered: Here I am. I am with you, Moses, I am with you. I am you just like you are me. You are the light of my eyes, the breath of my soul, the sound of my existence. You are the fragrance of my shadow, and your heart beats to the rhythm of my heart. We are One, Moses ben Amram. We are One. And God spoke his name, Ehiyeh Asher Ehiyeh, 'I am that I am.'

"Michal, decide who you want to be. Follow Moses from mountain to mountain. From Horeb to Nebo. From God to God. You have traveled the same way to get here and you have not seen the mountains. You have walked the path without having trust. Travel back on this path. Breathe the landscape and know that Moses' footsteps live in the memory of the sand. His words are stored in the memory of the world, and if you want to hear them, then travel with your feeling to where you want to be. May peace be with you, wherever you go."

I felt the space next to me filling up with what remained of the night. The fire died down and I saw the day awaken and stretch itself with long shadows. The darkness of morning was chased away by the first rays of the sun that played across the rocks. I closed my eyes and sat there waiting for the light. Slowly, it crept over to me. It stroked my feet, my legs; it warmed my hands and my chest; lovingly, it passed over my eyes and my nose. I was hugged by the light. "I am you and you are me, Ehiyeh Asher Ehiyeh."

I remained sitting there until the whole world was lit. At the end of the morning, I heard footsteps approaching. It was David.

"Shalom, Bubeleh, are you coming?"

On the way back to Jerusalem, I took in everything I could see around me.

Do You Have Faith in Yourself?
Living the Sixth Code

My mind traveled back to the night on the mountain, and my understanding of the faith Moses had had and his story that the promised land is not found outside the body but inside the heart, if you are able to feel the force of faith in your heart.

The sixth code is understanding that you must first become what you want to be. The sixth code opens with the words: "I am love, abundance, and wisdom. I am all, I am that which I am."

Can you feel in your heart what you want to be, how-ever small it is? Can you feel yourself also being this? Can you feel the abundance of the wind when it caresses your hair? Can you feel the warmth of the sun when it enters your heart, and the touch of the rain when your mind is refreshed? Can you feel the love in your heart when you think of all that is good and beautiful on this earth? Can you feel the light of wisdom shining in your soul? That which you feel, you will become. As within, so without. As above, so below. Behind each form that you want lives a feeling. Hang on to that feeling.

The Abraham Code

The Law of Abundance

There is an outer law that leans on an inner law of life. There where the outer laws are reflections of cosmic laws of life, they are meaningful and have essence. There where they deviate through human projections, they lose their essence.

—JACOB SLAVENBURG

Jerusalem, Winter 1983

They were all at home. All of them. Every one. Anna, Abraham, Sarah, the children, and Ben. Ben was waiting for me at the street corner. His bear dangled from one hand. I encircled him in my arms. I lifted him with my love, rocked him, and hugged him while kissing his cheeks. "My Ben . . . what a lovely little guy you are. How wonderful it is to feel you secretly wiping your nose on my sleeve and feel your clever hands searching through the pockets of my coat. What a treat it is to see your roguish eyes sparkle and watch the twinkles in them mingle in their special moonlike color. One day when you are older, you will heal people, recover lost souls, and strengthen lives. Then you will start traveling, and your eyes will see strange, far-reaching things. On your journey to peace you will become acquainted with hunger and war, oppression and power. You will meet people who will despise the peacefulness in you and who will answer you with their hatred, because you show them the absence of who they are. Your love makes them feel how frozen their own hearts are and, very occasionally, you will teach one of them the code of forgiveness. Then you will save a life, and that is precisely why, my dear Ben, you are here. I will worry even though I know better. I will ask the nights to watch over you, and I will fold together my hands in prayer, asking that you will be guarded on your way. My breath will follow you wherever you may go, and with all my strength I will protect you against evil, because opposite peace stands betrayal with its many disguises. I am certain that your eyes will always find the good and that the light of peace and love will shine through your soul. People will recognize this in you, my dear Ben. This makes you who you are, because you descend from wise old men who know the heart of the world, and they will guard you on the path you tread. And bravely I will wait until your distant travels dissolve your shadows; I will not show you how heavy my heart has been without you. I hope from the bottom of my soul that perhaps, one fine day, Ben, you will get married. That you will learn to live love, make love to your wife at night, and hold your firstborn in your arms. I do not know what other things life has to offer you. I dare not travel into your future. Choosing not to know is also a choice. Celebrate your life, Ben. Celebrate it as high and as wide as you can. Celebrate it with me."

I was nudged aside because David wanted to hug Ben. He gave him a kiss, and together we walked into the street. Ben turned around, halted, and beckoned to someone behind him. David turned around and asked: "Are you waiting for someone? There is no one there!" I looked back and saw what Ben saw. And so we walked on. Ben, David, myself, the bear, and . . . Jeshua.

We were received with laughter, warm kisses, and clapping. Joy had briefly returned to Abraham's house. Anna read my eyes and I thanked her for all her care. She had known that I needed to be baptized before being allowed to climb the mountain. She looked at David and smiled once again. Abraham, too, looked at me. He came to stand in front of me and said: "I see new light in your eyes." He was right. That was how it felt. The codes lived in me. Day by day I felt them awaken more strongly within me. There was one code I still had to learn, and I was curious which code would complete my journey.

The Final Code

And you, my dear reader, I thank you for your patient eyes and mind that have followed me so far. Thank you for allowing my words to live in your life. For you, too, the time has come to spread your wings. Flying is effortless when you allow the breeze to take its course. Go and stand in the open, stretch out your winged arms, and let the air dry your tears, wash away your sorrow, and evaporate your guilt. You have flown long enough against the storms and squalls. If you dare, the wind will take you with it, and it will carry you. Which breeze are you seeking in your life? Do you choose the zephyr of wisdom or of healing? Are you searching for love or do you prefer quietude? Or are you waiting for the airstream of abundance?

The wind knows many directions. It is up to you to choose the right bearing. It is time. The right time. The first code has taught you that you are already everything. You and I are One. There is no difference between great and small. All desires are equal in the field of unity. It is up to you to decide whether you wish for large or small desires.

The laws of nature have effect because it is their job to do this, and also, to them it makes no difference who or what you are. So, if you dare, step into the field of endless possibilities and stretch out your wings. The second code will show you the way because it teaches you that you yourself choose which way to go. You can wait until the geese are ready to leave, and then fly with them. But where are you flying to? If you are wise, you will choose the direction of your desire because your passion lights your inner world. It knows the map of your existence, and it will effortlessly take you to the third code of who you are, what you want, and why you are alive. It will show you the lessons that the school of life has to offer you, so that you can fly on to mastery and dare to be the visible expression of your invisible soul.

On the same day that you are able to regard life as a learning school with lessons in strength and trust, you will land on the water and allow the seas to wash over you, so that everything that no longer belongs with you can drift away. Dissolve your burdens with the water, give it your sorrows and your past. The water knows what to do with them. You will notice that when you surface again with peace in your heart and tranquility in your soul, the current of love will await you, because it is the fifth code. It will embrace you and cherish you and carry you wherever you want to go. It will rock you and love you and not judge you, because it knows that you and it are One, and it will navigate you to the sixth code of truth and trust. You are allowed to be all that you wish to be, and if you continue to float on the ocean of trust, then yes, my friend, the last code automatically flows toward you.

The Abraham Code

The Code of Abraham was disclosed to me at a clock-maker's premises. It was an old shop with a wooden stair-case and a floor made of stone on which special signs were visible. In misted-up showcases resided the memory of new and lived-through times. Everything ticked and moved. Here and there a gong sounded. The dust on most of the clocks covered their markings, but their hearts could be clearly heard. The clockmaker's name was Ibra-him, from the house of Abraham. His shop, the shop of time, was located in Kiryat Arba, Hebron, on the West Bank. His graying dark hair was neatly combed back. His old muscular hands trembled slightly when he spoke but became firm when they worked upon the timepieces, with agile fingers terminating in nails black-rimmed from the oil and polish. He was handsome, this man. Handsomely old. With the aristocratic nose of a magician and the mustache of a wise gray fox.

I was mesmerized by all the clock hands and pendulums. Not one was the same; they were all different, except for the time. On the table stood tea glasses filled with warm honey, yogurt, cinnamon, and walnuts. He offered me a glass.

"Ibrahim, why am I here?" I asked him. "Why am I with you?"

"Time is life. If you have time on your side, it will bring you luck, because you need time in order to understand the code of abundance. Time is very useful. It brings good news and heals all wounds. Time is present everywhere and yet it is not tangible, visible, or audible, and it cannot be smelled, yet the effect of time is visible in the mirror of our existence. Our life has a time span, between two moments in history. We live our life according to the movement of the clock, and therefore the end meets the beginning. There are people who are able to travel in time.

The power of their imagination travels faster than the time in which they reside. From a different layer of time they gather knowledge and take it back with them. The world calls them seers or prophets without realizing that we all have this gift.

"People's souls are timeless, but the heart and the head are connected by time. Some people live in haste, others live slowly. Unfortunately, only a few of them live in the Now. Yet this is where the true meeting takes place; in the Now is the door to the field of abundance. This is the secret of time. The fulfillment of our desires knows no time—that is its secret.

"He who has awareness knows the power of time. Time is intended to travel in and to play with, to move forward or backward. The seeker who lives the codes will instinctively stop his inner time so as to enter the field of abundance. His heart's wish lies waiting in the future, and mastery teaches us to travel there and take it with us. But most people wait until it is time. Until the right time has come. They wait and do not understand that time is an illusion, because there is no time other than that which is made by human beings. We wait until the teacher of time tutors us to be able to stop the clock and open the door to unity. When we move through the door, we are met by speechlessness, submission, acceptance, and trust. When we have no sense of time, we are there where we want to be. At that moment we can plant our desire, our life seed, in the most fertile soil that mother nature offers us, because then we have arrived in the universal garden. Over there ticks God's clock. There you hear his heart telling the right time."

Ibrahim whispered: "Shshshshshsh, can you hear that? Can you hear the ticking of silence? Can you hear the heartbeat of the universe? It has no sound, it is a deep, quiet knowing. There, my child, is the place to plant your prayer. Not a prayer made up of the right words. No, it is more a prayer of feeling, a combination of spontaneous words that are the expression of what makes your heart tick. Tick, TOCK, tick, TOCK, tick, TOCK . . . in between the ticking inside you lives your soul. If you want to hear what it is saying, then listen to the clock of your heart, because it jumps up when you meet your desire. This feeling is your prayer. It is the code of your life, and the code ticks with each heartbeat that you live. By living your inner prayer, you live in the soul of that which is."

He laid a seed in my hand. I looked at it. It was the

smallest seed in the world. "With what prayer do you want to fill this mustard seed, Bubeleh, with what prayer? What lives in your heart that is the most precious of all? What is your highest good?"

I nodded and closed my hand around the seed. With the power of my imagination, I filled the seed with that which was the reason I had come into this life. He took me with him to the back of the shop. I saw a small garden with a tree of life, the same tree I had seen at Anna's place. Ibrahim asked me to close my eyes. "Travel into the future. Travel to the outcome of your desire, and fill your seed with the feeling that this image brings you. Then travel back in time to the present moment and fill the seed with the power of your heart, the faith of your soul, and the happiness of your mind. If you truly believe that all you need already is, then all you need to do is to plant your seed and let nature do its work."

My knees touched the ground. My hands dug under the tree's roots, and in the heart under her trunk I planted my seed. It was time. Time to live my desire. Now. In this moment, I made a timeless decision. Ibrahim saw that I was touched. I had met my soul. As if his words had imperceptibly lifted me up in the timeless silence, I had heard the prayer of my heart.

"Go on, Bubeleh, keep walking, fly along with life, dare to go on, plant what you want in the heart of timeless universal history." He fetched a large cushion and invited me to sit on it. He himself sat down on the grass and began to talk.

"Through Abraham, we, Muslims and Jews, are related. We have the same primordial father. I come from the house of Abraham. Abraham is not only the father of the Jews. He is the founding father of Judaism, Christianity, and Islam. Abraham ben Terah, his name be praised, was the son of the earth. He married Sarai, but her womb was barren. Her slave Hagar took her place and gave birth for her to Ismaël ben Abraham. Sarai could not bring herself to welcome her husband's firstborn into her house. Not having had a son of her own overwhelmed her when she set eyes on Ismaël, and she sent Hagar and her son from her house. Hagar fled into the desert, but God saved her life along the way. Hagar descended from the line of primeval mothers, and her son became the original father of all Arabs. From this line the prophet Mohammed was to be born and one day make his famous journey into heaven.

"Sarai was deeply saddened. She carried a large guilt in her heart, and on her search for enlightenment, she came across a woman, a la Que Sabe, who purified her heart and soul and taught her how to travel through time to plant her precious desire to have a son. She learned to stop time, hear the prayer of her heart, and make this desire known to the soul of All that is. She returned to the village under a new name, Sarah. When her memory had almost forgotten her desire, she gave birth to her son Isaac. She enfolded him in her heart, surrounding him with love. On the day that Abraham took her child with the intention of sacrificing him, she laid her hands on the earth and begged mother nature to save her child. Abraham took his son to a place east of the old city of Jerusalem, on Mount Moriah, Har Habayit. He wanted to serve his creator unconditionally. The task that lay ahead of him was the most difficult of all time. It was the code of trust and submission. He took his son and placed him on a stone so as to kill him as a sacrifice. Just like Isa, whom you call Jeshua, Isaac was willing to give his life. He was small and brave, and he had unconditional faith in his father. When the soul of the world heard the prayer of submission, it saved that which was most precious to Abraham, and gave him the code of abundance, and spoke: 'You are not the instrument, but I am. I am the music that you can play. I am at your service. My strength and my laws are at the service of all that lives. How can I help you? It is a law of life that I must fulfill that which is most precious to you.'

"The place where God gave his promise to Abraham became the place of abundance: 'Where there are two, there is one.' This was where the most sacred places of Judaism and the Islamic sanctuary were to come together from the desert, as two brothers of the same primordial father, Ismaël and Isaac. Above this place God hung his cord of abundance, Habl Allah, a long line that would connect the descendents of Adam and Eve with eternity. The hand of God held the cord, and the cord itself became the link between his power and all the people on the earth, in unity and abundance. Those who saw the cord in their dreams made a heavenly journey to their own hearts and climbed upward within themselves along the laws and codes of existence. On that day, God gave Abraham a box with the seal of the prophets on it. In the box was hidden a big secret, the secret of creation. The box traveled the long line of prophets throughout history. The prophet Mohammed took it back to this land from a monastery, Pairs, situated in Bosra in Syria. He was young. The same young age as Jeshua when his uncle Aboe Talib took him to a teacher of the spiritual teaching school, Bahira. Sergious, his teacher, was the one who would initiate him in the codes. The box with the seal of the prophets would be passed down from teacher to student. This is how it had been for centuries. The box found its way via teachers from all corners of the world. It is locked, not with a key but with a word. He who knows the word can discover the knowledge, because nothing is secret that will not be made known."

He looked up at a high shelf in the shop. So high that a ladder was needed to reach it. I followed his gaze and saw a beautiful box, a box with black and red colors. Ibrahim noticed me looking at the box, and he nodded in confirmation. "It is the box with the seal of the prophets. No one is able to open it. There is no key, unless you know the code that is held in the box. Nothing other than your own heart can disclose the code to you."

Ibrahim had been given the box by his father, with the instruction never to sell it. His father had received it from a la Que Sabe from the area near Bethlehem, together with an assignment. What this assignment was, his father had never told him. He could only pass it on to the visitor who knew the answer to the question. He climbed up the steps, took the box, and placed it between us.

"Now you have been sent so that you would discover the seventh code."

The beat of my heart stopped for a moment because on the box I recognized Abraham's seal. Was that the reason I had been sent here by Abraham?

"Ibrahim, do you know the code?"

"No, I don't know it. My father did, though. According to tradition, the code is alternately known by men and women from the house of Abraham. The pendulum of the future has indicated a woman. It will be up to her to take back the box to our family on the other side. She will know the code so that the youngest of the family can inherit the box. A special task awaits him, and his inheritance will change the world."

What could the code be? What would the last code hold? I closed my eyes, and the voice of the story woman became audible. She softly whispered inside my head: "Think of Ben. Think of his gratitude and the naturalness with which he trusts life. His child's soul knows that everything already is and that in this universe there lives a word that contains a commandment to God."

My heart filled with warmth because I thought back to Ben's light, childish voice. Each night before jumping into bed he gave thanks for everything that his young life had met that day, from his bear to the cookies, from his Ima in heaven to his father on earth. He ended his prayer with the oldest word in the universe. The wisest word in the universe with the message of gratitude because everything already was. I whispered Ben's saying—"Aahhmenn." I heard a click and the box sprang open. Ibrahim led me to the door. I held the box under my arm and knew what I should do now. In the box were seeds from the tree of life. The oldest tree in the world. I understood that it was written in the stars that Ben would be planting his seeds of peace over the entire world. The choice was his. He could choose to marry, and to meet his children. He could choose to live his code and to spread out his seeds filled with peace throughout the world. He would walk in Jeshua's footsteps and go where no one had dared to go. I knew what he would choose and that I would have to be brave and should never stand in the way of his choice. His story had been written by him, the choice had been made, and I would live the Code of Miriam with love in my heart. But all that was in the future, for now he had a childhood to live. I could return the box to his father, Abraham, for safekeeping until it was time for Ben to live his code.

Ibrahim put his hands on my head. I knew that he could read my heart. He gave me the blessing of Moses.

"May Yahweh bless and protect you. May Yahweh let his light shine over you and keep you safe. May Yahweh be in your life, and may peace always be with you. Amen."

What Is Your Prayer?

There is a law in this universe that teaches us that gratitude brings the fulfillment of our desires. Amen, so be it, is a law. It is a code word. We give thanks when we receive something, using the word *amen*. Ending your prayer with the word *amen* means that you are certain and live in complete trust that you are making the connection between that which you want and that which you are. Everything already is. The codes know the way. Amen.

Epilogue

Nes aan de Amstel, Summer 2008

My Bubeleh,

This is my last letter to you. It will reach you when the time is right.

Years ago you asked me a question that I answered with painful honesty. All these years I have carried your question with me. My life gave me satisfaction, but my heart sometimes felt burdened, and in the same way I may have burdened your life. Last night I thought back to my life and understood that you are now my teacher and I am your student. Early this morning I was awakened by a bright light illuminating my room. I saw my son, our son. Ben, the child of us all. He smiled, took my hands, and spoke these two words: Thank you.

It was not a good-bye, but a reunion. His life flowed into my soul and made the last feelings of guilt and the last doubts disappear. Forgive me, Bubeleh, and do not *feel burdened any longer. I have found my last code and answered the last question you asked me.*

I have forgiven myself.

Sometimes we do not see the greater whole and do not understand the sacrifice. There is no blame. Rebecca knew that Ben had to be born. Like a tigress she fought for his life. She knew the risk involved, but she consciously chose to take that risk. She knew who her son was to become and saw the message that lay stored in his heart. Just like her mother, Rebecca possessed the wisdom of insight. Her Ben was to carry the code of peace and forgiveness, just like she had carried the code of love. She taught me to look further, further into the world so that the greater plan could become visible. We people have two eyes with which we can see, but if we learn to look with our hearts, we will meet the helmsman of the world. Life is greater than we sometimes think.

Thanks, my Bubeleh, for all you have done. Look with your heart and you will understand everything.

Abraham

Dear Rebecca, my dearest Abraham,

This morning Sarah gave me your last letter. It lay waiting in a cupboard, and I know that you will hear my words, the breeze will take them to you. In that I trust. They are the most difficult words I have ever written. They feel cold and empty, but the space between the letters tells their story.

Last week David and I received the message that Ben had died. The silence preceded the message. Missing him changed to worry, and the night before receiving the letter, I saw Ben's Jeshua by the side of my bed. Then I knew.

His ashes are on their way home. He was found in India. The cause of his death is not known, but he was found near a sacred place, high up in the mountains. He had already been dead for some days when they found him. The authorities, according to local custom,

cremated him. They did not know he was Jewish. It
does not matter anyway. He was a child of nature, and
we will plant his ashes near the tree in our back garden.

He would like that. The tree of life was precious to
him. It was the place where he sought quietude when he
came back from his long journeys.

My dearest Abraham, when he received the box
from the notary after you had passed away, he imme-
diately recognized the seal of the prophets. I have
often stood looking in admiration at how you put the
seal on your writings. I knew that you used it only
when you were passing on knowledge from the line
of teachers, so that the seal would protect the one
who received it and also protect the words. I watched
as Ben's hand stroked the box. It was a signal that
he understood how important the contents were.
He knew the code of the box. I do not know how he
knew, because I never told him. But when his hands held
the box given by the notary, he spoke the code. The
box opened and the light illuminated the seeds of the
tree of life. He recognized the seeds immediately. No
one had told him. It had not been necessary any-
way, because Ben was someone who was born from

the line of those who knew. He knew how precious the seeds were. That day I told him that for centuries the family had passed on the seeds, so that the knowledge would be safeguarded. That from father to son the seeds had been planted with what the world needed most. From Abraham to Ibrahim and onward.

When Ben and I moved to the Netherlands, together we planted a seed in the back garden. The tree became his best friend. I cannot count the hours that he slept under its branches. The box stands in his room. I am waiting for his ashes to arrive; then we can plant his memory together with a new seed in the garden of our lives.

I am writing to you with the request to welcome him. Search for him between the stars and take him with you to the light. I am confident that he is already with you, but I could not bear the thought of him wandering in the darkness.

We were used to Ben's journeys, his dissolving into life and somewhere being sheltered in love. We knew that his travels were strange and far, even at an early age.

*Dear Rebecca, as you had requested, David took
Ben with him on his twelfth birthday. A week earlier
I had already received a call from his teacher, his
Bahira, who told me that Ben was ready for his journey
through life. From that week on, Ben was receiving lessons that I could read in his eyes. During the holidays,
his teacher took Ben with him on trips that he could not
talk about. I understood because I had also made the
journey. As he got older, he traveled on inner and outer
journeys, and sometimes it seemed as if he could effortlessly travel through God's worlds, from the heavens to
the depths of the abyss and everything in between. Ben
was not of this world, but he lived in it nevertheless.
In God's garden he planted seeds with peace in places
where peace had been forgotten. I knew that I had
only borrowed Ben and that the day would come when
I had to let go of him. Without his knowledge, in my
imagination, I traveled ahead in time so as to have him
return safely. I was taught how to do this by Tibetans.
Tibetans imagine the safe return of all their loved ones,
as a sign of farewell. I did it all those years, except for
when Ben went to India. He had not told me about his*

departure. I found a letter on my desk. Had it been pre-destined that we were not to say good-bye to each other?

I hope to meet him in my dreams, at unexpected moments or somewhere along life's way. I will have to find the strength somehow to color the days and live life again joyfully.

Dear Rebecca, please give me a sign that you have found him. So that I know that he is safe. Ben lives on. He lives in our hearts. We miss him deeply, but his joy is greater. I will celebrate his life because Ben loved life too much to let people mourn for him or remember him in sorrow. I celebrate his laughter and his beauti-ful eyes, colored by the light of the moon. His poignant scent is carefully stored in the memory of my heart. I have not forgotten anything. Nothing whatsoever. Not a single detail. I will inter him near the tree and await new life, and one day, someday, I will be able to caress his branches.

New days will come with new light. I will wait for spring and the blossoming warmth that will dry my tears. I will wait until I receive the first sign from him. That is what I am waiting for.

Dear Abraham, now more than ever I give thanks for the fact that I know the codes. For how lonely is life for those who do not know what they form part of. How lost one must feel to live in a life where only that which you see exists and in which the beginning never meets the end. Abraham, the codes are ready just as you asked me. My thanks for your lessons, wondrous teachers, unexpected dreams, and the special journey. You will be glad to know that in the cupboard in Ben's room his writings are kept carefully. There are many manuscripts, and I am waiting for the day when I receive a sign telling me what I should do with them. Until the time is right, I will guard them with love. They carry the seal of the prophets and are filled with messages of great magnitude. I suspect that they relate to the choices the world will make. The layers of time store various possibilities; each choice has a different outcome. These are hidden until the world chooses between peace and light or fear and darkness.

Thank you, my dear friends, for letting Ben live in my life. I have cared for him with love, for who he was, but also for what his code stands for. Ben is the code for the best in us. He carries the frequency of love and freedom, but the most important message of Ben's life is peace. Ben was in love with life, and life was in love with him. All human beings carry a Ben within themselves. He is the child who believes in that which is good, the innocence in each human being. He is the compassion for ourselves and our empathy for others. He is the ability to live life in love and find happiness.

There is a story that a son would be born on earth who would bring love and release the world from evil. History has decided differently. The sun died on the symbol of his faith. But die he could not. And on the day that the world mourned for the illusion of his farewell, he returned with the message of peace. He was not able to leave. He was the face of unity, and the code of his story is that he would live on as Ben, a child of peace, in the hearts of people without guilt, in innocence.

Now the world is once again waiting. For a new Messiah, an Anointed One, a redeemer who will ban evil from the world. It was Ben's mission to show the world that the Messiah lives in each human being, that no one but us will come to heal the world. Each human being has the potential to be a Ben, and this is what we carry in our hearts and recognize in the outside world. Peace meets peace when we live in peace on an inner level. As within, so without. As above, so below. Ben was the carrier of the code of peace, and when we allow Ben's code to awaken in our hearts, peace will awaken on earth. A peaceful world is made up of peaceful people, just like a green forest is so by the grace of green trees. I will wait until Ben sends a signal to me. I will search heaven for an extra light among the stars, but meanwhile I will carry the light of his peace in my heart and feel Ben's strength.

I am copying the prayer of Ben among the stars. He wrote this prayer in his unfledged handwriting, on the wall of his childhood bedroom:

"Hello, dear night. Hello, beautiful stars. Hello, God and all sweet angels. Hello, all people of the world.

"My name is Ben and I am glad to be alive. Amen."
Love, more than love. Until the next time.

Your Michal

THE END

Thanks to the Reader

Ben is buried in the history and the future of who we are. We are Ben. We are peace, and the story of Ben is an appeal to find peace in your heart, quietude in your soul, and happiness in your mind. When we tune in to the frequency of unity and connection, we sense the child in ourselves awakening. The child who wants to share, who wants to play with life. The child who sees the world as a large and peaceful playground with an infinite field of possibilities in which there is enough of everything.

Thank you for your mindfulness. I hope that this book has helped you to open your heart and that you were able to receive it in gratitude. You know the code word of life. The word that teaches us that everything already is, because it has always been and will always be. The word carries the law of gratitude. We give thanks for all that we are a part of. We then say amen.

Plant peace together with whomever you want to be in the garden of your heart. Cherish it with your love, water it with your loyalty, and protect it with your faith. Ban any doubts and thank whomever you wish to thank for your happiness with the code word *amen*. Thank you for reading this far. May peace accompany you wherever you go, and may the codes cover you like a warm coat.

Good-bye, dear fellow human being, until a next time.

Patty Harpenau
Michal bat Abraham

Interested in
Knowing More?

Patty Harpenau is a trainer and coach and the author of various books on human nature. *The Life Codes* was written as a result of a special training she gives. During this training she personally initiates the Life Codes and the frequency and visualization exercises that form part of it. If you are interested in applying the exercises from the Life Codes within your own life, go to www.thelifecodes .com, where you can also order a companion audio workbook. In the workbook are exercises that correlate to each day of the week, along with additional information. At the site you will also find the visualization exercises described in this book. Each code has its own visualization training that can be downloaded for free.

The Life Foundation educates trainers who are interested in passing on the Life Codes. Further information can be found at www.thelifecodes.com and www.thelife foundation.nl. If you have any questions, send a message to info@thelifefoundation.nl.

To e-mail Patty Harpenau directly, send your message to pattyharpenau@thelifefoundation.nl.

A Word of Thanks

Good-bye, dear Ben. Thank you for wanting to live in my book. Thank you, dear Rebecca, for letting your words live in this book. Thank you, Abraham, for teaching me the codes and for letting your wisdom carry me. Thank you, old and new teachers of the world, for your knowledge, strength, and inspiration. I thank all the wondrous dreams and insights that have crossed my path; you have become the glue between my words.

I would like to express my love and gratitude to the following people: Rebecca Winfield for making my dreams come through. Amy Hertz and all the people at the Penguin Group who have helped let this book be born. My love is great for Laura Stadler, Stephanie Mason, and Jose de Boer.

Love and thanks to my best friends, my family, and all my staff at The Life Foundation in the Netherlands for their inspiration and commitment. Thanks to those who live in other times but are always with us. Thanks to my wonderful and beautiful sons, Dotan and Noam. But above all, I would like to thank God for letting me live life in love and abundance.

Amen.

Glossary

Abba—father

Bahira—prophet, monk

Bat—daughter

Ben—son

Bubeleh—sweetheart

Hashem—Hebrew synonym for God

Ima—mother

Ish—man

Isha—woman

Kosher—food in accordance with the rules of Jewish law

Rav—Rabbi

Sefer Yetzirah—the book of creation disclosed by God to Abraham

Sophia—feminine energy of God

Torah—Old Testament

Yeshiva—school where the Torah is taught